60¢

D1072852

AMERICA IS TOO YOUNG TO DIE

AMERICA IS TOO YOUNG TO DIE

Leonard Ravenhill

Bethany Fellowship INC.
MINNEAPOLIS, MINNESOTA 55438

Copyright © 1979
Leonard Ravenhill
All rights reserved

Published by Bethany Fellowship, Inc.
6820 Auto Club Road, Minneapolis, Minnesota 55438

Printed in the United States of America

Library of Congress Cataloging in Publication Data

Ravenhill, Leonard.
    America is too young to die.

    1. Christianity—United States—Miscellanea.
2. Church renewal—Miscellanea.   I. Title.
BR526.R38   262'.001   79-19229
ISBN 0-87123-013-5

Dedication

Frank Emerson Harris
Founder President
of
Homemakers Guild of America Corporation
Friend of God
Friend of Preachers
Friend of Mine

Other books by the author:

LEONARD RAVENHILL was born in 1907 in the city of Leeds, in Yorkshire, England. After his conversion to Christ, he was trained for the ministry at Cliff College. It soon became evident that evangelism was his forté and he engaged in it with both vigor and power. Eventually he became one of England's foremost outdoor evangelists. His meetings in the war years drew traffic-jamming crowds in Britain, and great numbers of his converts not only followed the Saviour into the Kingdom, but into the Christian ministry and the world's mission fields. In 1939, he married an Irish nurse, and from that union have come three sons. Paul and David are themselves ministers of the gospel, and Phillip is a teacher. Leonard and his wife now live near Lindale, Texas, from which place Ravenhill travels to widely scattered preaching points in conference ministry.

Foreword

When Ahab decided to go up against Ramoth-gilead, he invited Jehoshaphat to join him. The king of Judah suggested that they seek the approval of the clergy, so four hundred false prophets were called. The prophets said in unison, "Go up and prosper." That sounded too unanimous to Jehoshaphat; he asked, "Is there not here a prophet of the Lord *besides*, that we may inquire of him?" Ahab replied that there was one odd number whom he hated because "he testifieth not good concerning me but evil." (Joseph Parker said, "The world always hates the four-hundred-and-first prophet.")

Leonard Ravenhill is a prophet 401 today. He defies classification in the clerical catalog, as true prophets have always done. We have never been over-supplied with true prophets, although pastors, evangelists and teachers abound. The school of Micaiah has never been regimented, standardized in assembly-line production. Ravenhill speaks for God to the Nation and to the Church. He is not impressed by the status quo or satisfied with things as they are. He rides no bandwagon shouting, "On to Ramoth-gilead," although its promoters may justify the venture by quoting scripture as Ahab could have done.

It is a sad day for any nation when there is no Amos in

Bethel. The times today are not unlike the days of the "troubler" from Tekoah. All the evils Amos thundered against abound in America. Jeroboam sets up an easy religion—"It is too much for you to go up to Jerusalem." Dr. Amaziah, the court preacher, bids the fig-pincher go back whence he came. But Amos had one thing going for him— he had heard from heaven.

Leonard Ravenhill walks in the succession of those who are grieved for the affliction of Joseph. His message is the prophetic trumpet blast, not a pep talk at the civic club. As in the days of Ezekiel there are those who may come out and sit and hear and do nothing about it. But the final verdict will be that a prophet has been among them. This book will not be a favorite with those who cry, "Peace," when there is no peace; but it will be welcomed by all who inquire in these troubled days, "Is there not a prophet of the Lord *besides*, that we may inquire of him?"

Dr. Vance Havner

Author's Preface

This book has not been written with an eye on the cash register. I get no financial return from it. Neither has it been written for fun or to add yet another book to my list of writings. It has been written with grief and bathed in prayer. It is written with love for the land of my adoption.

For the last fifty years I have watched Great Britain decay during her lingering agony of alternating fits of sanity and of stupefaction. Today England is no longer considered a world power. Most say that she is both morally and spiritually decadent. Must the United States follow her? I pray not. We are considered by most folk to be on the skids. Our dollar is sick. Our morality is sick. At two o'clock one morning a man called me and tearfully sobbed, "Ravenhill, I am just reading *Why Revival Tarries*, and I found out three things: my Nation is sick, my church is sick, and I am sick."

These are the last days—how long will they last? God has a remnant. He calls us to battle principalities and powers. "Lead on, O King Eternal," cleanse us and heal our land.

I am deeply grateful to Brad and Estelle Jackson for their fine work in editing this manuscript. Theirs is an unpaid task which they do cheerfully and with accuracy. I appreciate this devotion.

Leonard Ravenhill

Contents

I Walked Today

I walked today as Dante walked
In days of long ago;
I gasped through stench of this earth's hell;
The air was filled with woe.
Men scarred with sin, in rags, ill shod,
   Their face blank in despair,
   Their livid eyes burned into me—
   My joy turned into misery.
   I cried, "O Christ of Calvary,
Awake Thy church to care!"

I walked today where Christ would walk
If He were here on earth;
The air was thick with discontent
And total lack of mirth.
   It seemed despair had carved each face;
   And greed and lust and vice,
   Like chains, had bound resentful men.
   "And, Lord," I asked, "oh when, oh when
   Will Thy dear church revive again
To seek Thy power in prayer?"

I walked today mid cultured vice,
And as I walked, I wept.
I thought, Lord, of Thy sacrifice
And how Thy church has crept
   Along the road this past decade
   And slumbered in soft pews,
   While millions in their sinful plight
   Fall into hell's eternal night.
   O Christ, in mercy purge our blight;
Anoint Thy church to tell!

—Leonard Ravenhill

(Written after a visit to a drug area in a large city.)

Chapter 1

Amos Goes to Washington

Amos 6

1. Woe to them that are at ease in Washington and trust in bureaucracy and the power of the dollar, chiefs of this most powerful race, to whom the people of America look.

2. Pass over to London, and see; and from there go you to Moscow the great; then go down to Rome of the Italians: are you really better than these lands, as you so often boast?

3. You that put off the day of reckoning, being indifferent toward immorality, and lawlessness, and creeping anarchy (even some of your chief religious leaders seem to endorse sexual license, while some are heralding the death of God);

4. That lie upon mattresses, which to sleep on is like sleeping on a cloud, and grow over-fat on too much rich food while you loll in overstuffed chairs hearkening to trivia on TV;

5. That writhe like tormented savages to the weird sound of guitars played by long-haired murderers of music;

6. That drink wine and martinis, stingers and grasshop-

pers, that smoke longer and longer cigarettes (although the medics warn they may cause lung cancer), and are not grieved for the affliction of the young men in Viet Nam or for the youth heading for anarchy in the Nation.

7. Therefore shall the prices of commodities rise higher and higher with encroaching inflation, and your banquets be taken away by reason of the population and world famine.

8. The Lord has sworn by himself, "I abhor the pride of America; therefore will I deliver up the country with all its senators and congressmen and those who ride on political coattails."

9. And it shall come to pass that if there remain ten men in one house, they shall all die; for the thermo-nuclear power of the foe is great, even as your own.

10. And if some survivor brings the bodies from the rubble for cremation, and cries, "Are there any left alive?" and one shall say, "No," then shall he say, "Let us grieve silently; for we were forbidden to pray in the classroom, and now we may not mention God's name."

11. Behold, the Lord commands, and the White House shall be smitten, and the little houses shattered.

12. Shall Cadillacs race over boulders? or tractors plow in rock? For you have turned my Word into a myth, and the fruit of righteousness into "pot" and LSD.

13. You who rejoice in nothing, and say, "We defeated the Nazis by our own strength and will build the Great Society by our own ingenuity; by our technocratic know-how we will bring peace and plenty in the earth."

14. "Behold, I will raise up against you nation after nation, O house of Washington," says the Lord the God of hosts; "and they shall afflict you from the United Nations to Viet Nam."

Amos 7:10, 12-17

10. Then Amaziah, the far-out liberal at Washington who had jettisoned the Apostles' Creed, sent word to the President, saying, "Amos has conspired against you, for he is a dangerous right-winger and extremist, and the country is not able to bear his words."

12. Also Amaziah said unto Amos, "O you dreamer! Be off to the Ozarks and eat cornbread there, and do your preaching there:

13. "But preach no more in Washington, for it is the seat of the bureaucrats and the headquarters for the Nation."

14. Then answered Amos and said unto Amaziah, "I was not a preacher, not even a seminarian; nor was my father a preacher or a seminarian; but I was a sheep-herder and fruit-picker, without so much as membership in a union.

15. "And the Lord took me from the flock, and said, 'Go and preach to my people America.'

16. "Now therefore hear the word of the Lord: You say, 'Do not preach against America, and drop not your word against the house of Washington.'

17. "Therefore thus says the Lord: 'Your wife shall become immoral in suburbia, and your sons and daughters shall be swallowed up in riots; you shall lose your common stock and your preferred holdings, and you shall die in a land polluted by Communism. And America shall fall captive to dark circumstances beyond her control.' " *

---

*Written by Lon Woodrum in 1967 in *Christianity Today.* Quoted by kind permission.

The prophet is a man of deep pathos in the classic sense of the word, which means "suffering." He suffers with his people, for his people, and because of his people. *Above all, he suffers with God and for God*, because sin and unrighteousness alienate the people from their holy God. (Italics mine.)
—Dr. Victor Buksbazen

Oh, ye white-faced, weak-kneed believers! Believers in what? Ye shifty speculators, stealers of prophetic mantles! go, drink yourselves to death, and go to your proper devil! Ye are not the church of Christ, might well be the speech which ascended Pauls might deliver to us, as we reshuffle the theological cards, and rearrange our credenda, and modify and dilute our doctrinal positions and enthusiasms.
—Dr. Joseph Parker

Our pulpits today are occupied with puppets rather than with prophets, with organizers rather than with agonizers.
—Leonard Ravenhill

Chapter 2

Picture of a Prophet

The prophet in his day is fully accepted of God and totally rejected by men.

Years back Dr. Gregory Mantle was right when he said, "NO man can be fully accepted until he is totally rejected."

The prophet of the Lord is aware of both of these experiences. They are his "brand name."

The group challenged by the prophet because they are smug and comfortably insulated from a perishing world in their warm but untested theology are not likely to vote him "man of the year" when he refers to them as habituates of the "synagogue of Satan"!

The prophet comes to set up that which is upset. His work is to call into line those who are out of line!

He is unpopular because he opposes the popular in morality and spirituality.

In a day of faceless politicians and voiceless preachers, there is not a more urgent national need than that we cry to God for a prophet!

The function of the prophet, as Austin Sparks once said, "has almost always been that of recovery."

The prophet is God's detective seeking for lost spiritual

treasures. The degree of his effectiveness is determined by the measure of his unpopularity.

Compromise is not known to him.

He has no price tags.

He is totally "otherworldly."

He is unquestionably controversial and unpardonably hostile.

He marches to another drummer!

He breathes the rarefied air of inspiration.

He is a "seer" who comes to lead the blind.

He lives in the heights with God and comes into the valley with a "thus saith the Lord."

He shares some of the foreknowledge of God, and so is aware of impending judgment.

He lives "in splendid isolation."

He is forthright and outright, but he claims no birthright.

His message is "repent, be reconciled to God or else . . . !"

His prophecies are parried.

His truth brings torment, but His voice is never void.

He is the villain of today and the hero of tomorrow.

He is excommunicated while alive and exalted when dead!

He is dishonored with epithets when breathing and honored with epitaphs when dead.

He is a schoolmaster to bring us to Christ, but few "make the grade" in his class.

He is friendless while living and famous when dead.

He is against the "establishment" in ministry; then he is established as a "saint" by posterity.

Daily he eats the bread of affliction while he ministers, but he feeds the Bread of Life to those who listen.

He walks before men for days, but has walked before God for years.

He is a scourge to the nation before he is scourged by the nation.

He announces, pronounces, and denounces!

He has a heart like a volcano and his words are as fire.

God talks to him about men.

He talks to men about God.

He carries the lamp of truth amongst heretics while he is lampooned by men.

He faces God before he faces men, but he is self-effacing.

He hides with God in the "secret place," but he has nothing to hide in the marketplace.

He is naturally sensitive but supernaturally spiritual.

He has passion, purpose and pugnacity.

He is "ordained" of God but disdained by men.

Our national need at this hour is not that the dollar recover its strength, or that we save face over "the Watergate Affair," or that we find the answer to the ecology problem. We need a God-sent prophet!

I am bombarded with talk or letters about the coming shortages in our national life: bread, fuel, energy. I read between the lines from people not practiced in scaring folk. They feel that the "seven years of plenty" are over for us. The "seven years of famine" are ahead.

But the greatest famine of all in the Nation at this given moment is a FAMINE OF THE HEARING OF THE WORDS OF GOD (Amos 8:11).

Millions have been spent on evangelism in the last twenty-five years. Hundreds of gospel messages streak through the air over the Nation *every day*. Crusades have been held, healing meetings have made a vital contribution, "come outers" have "come out" and settled, too, without a Nation-shaking revival. Organizers we have, skilled preachers abound, multi-million dollar Christian organizations straddle the Nation. BUT where, oh where, is the prophet? Where are the incandescent men fresh from the Holy Place? Where is the Moses to plead in fasting before the holiness of the Lord for our moldy morality, our political perfidy, and sour and sick spirituality?

GOD'S MEN ARE IN HIDING UNTIL THE DAY OF THEIR SHOWING FORTH. They will come.

The prophet is violated during his ministry, but he is vindicated by history.

There is a terrible vacuum in Evangelical Christianity today. The missing person in our ranks is the prophet. The man with a terrible earnestness. The man totally otherworldly. The man rejected by other men, even other good men, because they consider him too austere, too severely committed, too negative and unsociable.

Let him be as plain as John the Baptist.

Let him for a season be a voice crying in the wilderness of modern theology and stagnant churchianity.

Let him be as selfless as Paul the apostle.

Let him, too, say and live, "This ONE thing I do."

Let him reject ecclesiastical favors.

Let him be self-abasing, nonself-seeking, nonself-projecting, nonself-righteous, nonself-glorying, nonself-promoting.

Let him say nothing that will draw men to himself, but only that which will move men to God.

Let him come daily from the throne room of a holy God, the place where he has received the order of the day.

Let him, under God, unstop the ears of the millions who are deaf through the clatter of shekels milked from this hour of material mesmerism.

Let him cry with a voice this century has not heard because he has seen a vision no man in this century has seen. God send us this Moses to lead us from the wilderness of crass materialism, where the rattlesnakes of lust bite us and where enlightened men, totally blind spiritually, lead us to an ever-nearing Armageddon.

God have mercy; send us PROPHETS!

THOMAS MACAULAY, the British historian who died on the eve of our Civil War, wrote a warning to America. He predicted the possibility that our country would come under a dictatorship. The alternative which he forecast is no less foreboding. Macaulay wrote *" . . . your republic will be fearfully plundered and laid waste by barbarians in the Twentieth Century as the Roman Empire was in the Fifth, with this difference: that the Huns and Vandals who ravaged the Roman Empire came from WITHOUT and your Huns and Vandals will have been engendered WITHIN your own country, by your own institutions."*
—Dr. Kenneth McFarland

Chapter 3

America Is Too Young To Die

Compared with hoary dynasties and the empires of the ages, America is but a prattling child in a crib playing with its toes. Compared with the ancient civilizations, America was born only yesterday. But, and here is the rub, she is dying today, and she will be dead tomorrow unless there is a spiritual awakening.

After the great spiritual revival of the nineteenth century, America ran ahead of the other nations. Fugitives from injustice and from the crippling bondages of poverty, superstition, and oppression found their way to these shores.

Later, men fleeing the cruelty of dictators fled here for refuge. The Statue of Liberty testifies to the compassion of the American republic.

But now America is in the storm center of a fearful internal revolution, and she has no other alternative but to fear God and cleanse her heart.

Every sign on the television which says, "Where are your children just now?" should be followed with one that reads: "AMERICA IS IN DANGER!"; and it should be shown over and over until it has soaked into the national consciousness that this *is* the most critical hour in American history.

Listen to the voice of an American Great, speaking over a century ago.

"At what point, then, is the approach of danger to be expected? If it ever reaches us, it must spring up among us. It cannot come from abroad. If destruction be our lot, we must ourselves be its author and finisher; as a nation of freemen, we must live through all time or die by suicide."

So spake the great Abraham Lincoln.

Fifty years later, Theodore Roosevelt said, "The things that destroy America *are prosperity at any price, peace at any price, safety first instead of duty first, and love of soft living and the get-rich-quick theory of life."*

"Love that is pure is passionate," so says the old proverb. Passionate love for his country burns as fiercely in the heart of the seeing politician patriot as it does in the heart of the romantic lover.

Two centuries before Christ, Cato the Elder saw the corrupting influence of the Romans penetrating his beloved Greece, and his zeal to defend his country's culture turned him into one of the most eloquent and impassioned orators of history.

When the ideals of Greek civilization were threatened by barbarian violence, the same kind of passion carried Demosthenes to the height of majestic oratory in such a measure that his speeches decrying Greek indifference have served as models of perfection to students of rhetoric for centuries.

Patrick Henry's passionate—and pure—love for his country produced a speech whose conclusion has stirred the true American spirit for nearly two hundred years: "Give me liberty or give me death!"

But of all these orators, the British would say that none of them, not even Demosthenes, ever surpassed Edmund Burke. Fired as he was with passionate devotion to the British throne and empire, he fairly burst with unmitigated zeal against the atrocities perpetrated by Warren Hastings in India. Hastings had dragged the then fair name of Britain into the gutter. For four days, without so much as a note in his hand, Burke recited the cruelties he and others believed Hastings had committed in India. So powerful was his speech that Mrs. Sissons, then queen of the English stage, had to be carried out in a faint during the blazing oratory. Such was the description Burke painted, and so did he fire the hearts of his listeners.

His words were extreme, passionate, and straight to the point, and never more so than when he spoke of his beloved Britain. As far as I am concerned, he never soared higher than when he said, "Men are qualified for civil liberty in exact proportion to their disposition to put moral chains upon their own appetites . . . in proportion as their love of justice is above their rapacity . . . in proportion as their soundness and sobriety of understanding is above their vanity and presumption . . . in proportion as they are more disposed to listen to the counsels of the wise and good, in preference to the flattery of knaves. Society cannot exist unless a controlling power upon will and appetite be placed somewhere; and the less of it there is within, the more there must be without. It is ordained in the eternal constitution of things, that men of intemperate minds cannot be free. Their passions forge their fetters.

In a day when permissiveness is the unwritten law of millions, these pure words of an impassioned patriot ought to be trumpeted from one end of America to the other! In a day when men ignore the diagnosis of history and pretend that America does not have the disease that destroyed every major civilization there ever was, it is time to tell the truth with all the passion and zeal that pure love for one's country can produce!

America can die, but it would have to be by suicide. It would be because she thinks God is dead, and because she believes that His laws, which, when broken, have felled every nation that ever lived, do not, in her hour of freedom and affluence, include her.

America will not be sold by Alger Hiss or the Rosenburgs, but by people who just don't care.

America fights a battle that cannot be won at the ballot box. Her need is not the "new morality" of the hour, but new morals based on the old laws of God.

"These are the times that try men's souls," said Thomas Paine in one of his political works. Then with passion he wrote, "Tyranny, like hell, is not easily conquered; yet we have this consolation with us, that the harder the conflict, the more glorious the triumph." The task of getting America morally cleansed is not an easy one. But it is not an impossibility either.

It would be a good start to moral recovery and international prestige if we put the Bible back in the schools and the family altar back into our homes. Then let me suggest that those who have not read *The Death of a Nation* get a copy and read it. Follow that with *The Death of the Dollar*.

America needs a Joan of Arc. The British need another Boadicia to wage war on her immorality. Both nations need another Jeremiah to weep over their sins, another John the Baptist to call them to repentance, and another Elijah to bring fire down from heaven that the multitude may cry again, "The LORD, he is God! The LORD, he is God!"

Whittier wrote:

Is the old Pilgrim spirit quench'd within us?
Stoops the proud manhood of our souls so low,
That Mammon's lure or Party's wile can win us to si-
lence now?
Now, when our land to ruin's brink is verging.
In God's NAME LET US SPEAK WHILE THERE IS
TIME:
Now, when the padlocks for our lips are forging,
SILENCE IS A CRIME.

We go down to our knees, or we go down to oblivion. Then God himself will write for us the epitaph He wrote for Israel: "The Lord hath a controversy with the inhabitants of the land, because there is no truth, nor mercy, nor knowledge of God in the land. By swearing, and lying, and killing, and stealing, and committing adultery, they break out, and blood toucheth blood. Therefore shall the land mourn . . . therefore shalt thou fall in the day. . . . My people are destroyed for lack of knowledge. . . . I will also forget thy children."

That is a doom too bleak to accept. Let us go down to our knees. AMERICA IS TOO YOUNG TO DIE!

Chapter 4

Let's Stop Playing Church

Walter Lippmann gives the Church a crisp slap in the face when he scathingly says that we believers are a group of "grimly spiritual persons devoted to the worship of sonorous generalities." Is that statement palatable, or does it set our teeth on edge? That is Lippmann's cultured way of saying that we Christians are sleepwalkers, not aware of what is happening around us, nor conscious of the direction in which we are going. If he is wrong, we can laugh off his jibe; if he is right, we need to do some stocktaking.

This much is sure: this generation is mesmerized by materialism and tantalized by TV. It is jeopardized by evils no other age has known, and victimized by cruel, malicious propaganda that clouds reality and therefore confuses thinking. The last but not least ingredient of this "witches brew" is the religious jackanapes, attracting the crowd to his revival jamboree with the lure of miracles, as a cover-up for his itch for gold. What a day!

The enervated evangelism of the hour has left a trail of spiritual chaos. One of the top ten evangelists mourns that only half of one percent of his converts endure. Another declares that a year after their decision, not ten percent of converts show any sign of regeneration.

Out of their bondage, sorrow, and night, millions are crying for deliverance, for they are squeezed under the iron heel of Communism. Yet free men heed their cries with little concern. Never has God looked down on more millions in human misery than at this hour. Before our eyes the unbelievable happens. International burglars, that is, the Communist section of the U.N., have convened in New York to masterplan the way to rob the rest of the world of its freedom. When did a brood of evil men like Tito, Castro, Gomulka, Novotny, and Khrushchev ever stalk openly into another nation's front room and, while planning its rape, partake of its hospitality? Here are men treading ground sanctified to the freedom of the nations, yet planning world enslavement. Here in a multimillion-dollar palace dedicated to unity, these political perverts plan world disruption and division. This is unprecedented in political records.

Political maneuvering and adroitness may stave off world enslavement, but unless there is a Holy Ghost revival, it will only push it back for a breathing space. Concerning the crucifixion of Cuba, there has been among Christians more anger than agony, and we have yet to hear of nights of concentrated intercession for Cambodia's deliverance from communistic castigation. Apart from Holy Ghost breakings, what will ring the emergency bell in the church of the living God? When are we going to stop playing church?

Some see a star of promise in this sky of moral, political, and spiritual blackness. They declare with delight that before we can be enslaved by organized political evil, we shall at the last minute be raptured. Others are advocating the Christian gospel as a sure sign to prosperity. Why, then, were the saints in China who were subdued by Stalin not raptured? Why did God *seem* to stand by while Viet Nam and Cambodia were mutilated? Are we Western Christians a better breed and of better spiritual pedigree than they?

The enslaved might now be crying, "The harvest is passed; the summer is ended, and we are not saved." The people of Judah, who in times past did cry thus, heard Hosea's call, "Ephraim is joined to his idols: let him alone." They saw the northern folk taken into captivity. But they sinned against light. God warned them, Jeremiah warned them, calamity to other people warned them; but on they went to their doom of captivity and lived to eat their own offspring. Eleven times in this book of Jeremiah (more times than in any other book in the Bible) we read, "God rose up early." God *tried* to intervene. As they made their first steps to calamity, He called them—but all was to no avail. At such a time, "Thus saith the Lord, Let not the *wise* man glory in his wisdom, neither let the *mighty* man glory in his might, let not the *rich* man glory in his riches" (Jer. 9:23). But when there is danger around we are prone to do all three things. Yet brains can *not* help us out of the jam we are in.

God has a controversy with the nations. First, I believe, He has a controversy with His Church. As with Israel, so with us. We have substituted organizing for agonizing, and equipment for "enduement." The world is not even mildly interested in our gyrating. Jeremiah's roots were deep. Read the first few verses of his prophecy. There God says of Jeremiah, "*I formed thee . . . , I knew thee . . . , I sanctified thee . . . , I ordained thee . . . , I shall send thee . . . , I command thee . . . , I am with thee.*" Could Jeremiah ask for more?

My minister brethren, are we thus set about and buttressed with the exceeding great and precious promises of the Lord? The answer is a resounding yes—in this titanic end-time struggle we have the overweight of the finished work of Christ as well as the promise of Holy Ghost power for our commission.

I believe that at this hour the world is facing more solemn alternatives than she did on the eve of the Civil War. Few Americans doubt that this age needs a moral and spiritual revolution. No nation is better than its church, and no church is better than its people. Only God-transformed personalities can change the moral fiber of the Nation.

At the time of the fall of Jerusalem, the voice of God, the voice of Jeremiah, the passing of three kings (two of them led into captivity), and the bondage of the northern people—all stood in the path of the self-enslaving people of Judah. Today America, too, will have a tough time in committing spiritual suicide. What barriers are against her? There are so many that they seem informidable (but they are not). First, America must close her ears to more gospel broadcasts per day and per week than any other nation in the world. Next, she has to climb over a mountain of Bibles higher than the Great Divide. Then she must swim through a river of printers' ink, dedicated to the publication of tracts, books and periodicals, all calling her back to God. Certainly the endless belt of Bible conferences circling the Nation is no easy grip to escape.

Another blockade against America's bid for bondage is the fact that she has more men under "alms" than any other nation in the world. The Americans are hilarious givers and dole out largely and liberally for missions and world evangelism. Shall this Nation yet cry, "They made me the keeper of the vineyards; but mine own vineyard have I not kept"?

Finally, America is blest with more Bible propaganda

than any other nation and has more full-time and part-time preachers than half a dozen other nations put together.

This catalogue of divine favors makes stirring reading but is loaded with vast obligation, for America has the capacity to save herself *and* the world. The man with a loaded granery is obligated to feed the starving neighbors. We who have the awareness of the world peril and lateness of the hour are debtors to rescue what will otherwise be a lost cause and a perpetual blot on our spiritual history. Having the load of spiritual potential mentioned in this chapter, America can and must rise to write a new chapter in the history of the church of Jesus Christ.

Emergency situations call for emergency measures. The sweet hour of prayer as a mid-week breather in the church has been reduced to a sweet twenty minutes of prayer. We sing awhile, have a Bible reading, review the immediate program of the church, and then wind up with a conscience-salving twenty minutes for stating needs to God. Would to God that we could rise a battalion of wet-eyed intercessors for this hour of unprecedented grief and spiritual peril! The slogan of the Church must be, "We will give ourselves continually to prayer, and to the ministry of the word." *Every* church needs a prayer meeting *every* night of the week *right now*. Midday and all-day prayer meetings must be convened. God will welcome us putting Him to the test. How amazed He must still be that there are no intercessors! Denominational segregation must go; barriers must be eliminated and group prayer meetings formed. This is the crisis hour of the Church as well as the world. We must obey the Bible command to fast and pray, lest at the bar of God He says to us what He said to another, "Curse ye Meroz, said the angel of the Lord. Curse ye bitterly the inhabitants thereof; because they came not to the help of the Lord, to the help of the Lord against the mighty" (Judges 5:23). If we face up to the calamity of this hour, we shall get our faces down into the dust to cry, "Arm of the Lord, awake and put on strength!" Out of these protracted prayer times would come a people glowing and growing, plus a whole new crop of last-day prophets. Let's make no mistake—they will come!

I was stirred to my depths the other day in reading of J. N. Darby (founder of the Plymouth Brethren). He was an unctionized prophet. Born in England of Irish parents, he entered Trinity College, Dublin, as a fellow-commoner at fifteen years of age; and at a little more than eighteen years of age, he was a graduate with a classical gold medal. He entered the legal profession and was called to the Irish Chancery Bar. It seemed the road before him was paved with gold. Then God took over, for J. N. Darby was saved. Later he entered the Church of Ireland and was ordained a deacon by Archbishop Magee of Dublin. His was the life of a zealot. He roved over the bogs, moved in the Wicklow mountains, and was seldom home before midnight. Says one writer, "In an age of rampant materialism, the simplicity and frugality of his life rivaled that of the early saints. In middle life he trudged *on foot* through France and Switzerland. He subsisted at times on acorns, or welcomed a glass of milk and an egg for dinner as if it were a banquet." Newman says of Darby, "His bodily presence was indeed weak—a fallen cheek, a blood-shot eye, a crippled limb resting on a crutch, a seldom-shaved beard, a suit of shabby clothes and a generally neglected person." William Kelly adds, "Thoughtful for others, he was indifferent to comforts for himself. His clothes were plain, and he wore them to shabbiness."

This then is a stirring picture of the golden-brained man

who was at that time the Apostle to the Irish Catholics. According to the record of Neatby, he won them to Christ at the rate of 600 to 800 per week, to the consternation of all. Darby's apostolic method and apostolic result came out of his meeting for nights of prayer and meditation on the Word. God is all fire and all power, and He longs to baptize His blood-bought church with a baptism of fire and power—*that the world might know!*

THE PRAYER OF A MINOR PROPHET

This is the prayer of a man called to be a witness to the nations. This is what he said to his Lord on the day of his ordination. After the elders and ministers had prayed and laid their hands on him, he withdrew to meet his Saviour in the secret place and in the silence, farther in than his well-meaning brethren could take him.

And he said, O Lord, I have heard Thy voice and was afraid. Thou hast called me to an awesome task in a grave and perilous hour. Thou art about to shake all nations and the earth and also heaven, that the things that cannot be shaken may remain. O Lord, our Lord, Thou hast stopped to honor me to be Thy servant. No man taketh this honor upon himself save he that is called of God as was Aaron. Thou hast ordained me Thy messenger to them that are stubborn of heart and hard of hearing. They have rejected Thee, the Master, and it is not to be expected that they will receive me, the servant.

My God, I shall not waste time deploring my weakness nor my unfittedness for the work. The responsibility is not mine, but thine. Thou hast said, "I knew thee—I ordained thee—I sanctified thee," and Thou hast also said, "Thou shalt go to all that I shall send thee, and whatsoever I command all that I shalt speak." Who am I to argue with Thee or to call into question Thy sovereign choice? The decision is not mine, but Thine. So be it, Lord. Thy will, not mine, be done.

Well do I know, Thou God of the prophets and the apostles, that as long as I honor Thee Thou wilt honor me. Help me therefore to take this solemn vow to honor Thee in all my future life and labors, whether by gain or by loss, by life or by death, and then to keep that vow unbroken while I live.

It is time, O God, for Thee to work, for the enemy has entered into Thy pastures and the sheep are torn and scattered. And false shepherds abound who deny the danger and laugh at the perils which surround Thy flock. The sheep are deceived by these hirelings and follow them with touching loyalty while the wolf closes in to kill and destroy. I beseech Thee, give me sharp eyes to detect the presence of the enemy; give me understanding to distinguish the false friend from the true. Give me vision to see and courage to report what I see faithfully. Make my voice so like thine own that even the sick sheep will recognize it and follow Thee.

Lord Jesus, I come to Thee for spiritual preparation. Lay Thy hand upon me. Anoint me with the oil of the New Testament prophet. Forbid that I should become a religious scribe and thus lose my prophetic calling. Save me from the curse that lies dark across the face of the modern clergy, the curse of compromise, of imitation, of professionalism. Save me from the error of judging a church by its size, its popularity or the amount of its yearly offering. Help me to remember that I am a prophet; not a promoter, not a religious manager—but a prophet. Let me never become a slave to crowds. Heal my soul of carnal ambitions and deliver me from the itch for publicity. Save me from bondage to things. Let me not waste my days puttering around the house. Lay Thy terror upon me, O God, and drive me to the place of prayer where I may wrestle with principalities and powers and the rulers of the darkness of this world. Deliver me from overeating and late sleeping. Teach me self-discipline that I may be a good soldier of Jesus Christ.

I accept hard work and small rewards in this life. I ask for no easy place. I shall try to be blind to the little ways that could make my life easier. If others seek the smoother path I shall try to take the hard way without judging them too harshly. I shall expect opposition and try to take it quietly when it comes. Or if, as sometimes it falleth out to Thy servants, I should have grateful gifts pressed upon me by Thy kindly people, stand by me then and save me from the blight that often follows. Teach me to use whatever I receive in such manner that it will not injure my soul nor diminish my spiritual power. And if in Thy permissive providence honor should come to me from Thy church, let me not forget in that hour that I am unworthy of the least of Thy mercies, and that if men knew me as intimately as I know myself they would withhold their honors or bestow them upon others more worthy to receive them.

And now, O Lord of heaven and earth, I consecrate my remaining days to Thee; let them be many or few, as Thou wilt. Let me stand before the great or minister to the poor and lowly; that choice is not mine, and I would not influence it if I could. I am Thy servant to do Thy will, and that will is sweeter to me than position or riches or fame and I choose it above all things on earth or in heaven.

Though I am chosen of Thee and honored by a high and holy calling, let me never forget that I am but a man of dust and ashes, a man with all the natural faults and passions that plague the race of men. I pray Thee, therefore, my Lord and Redeemer, save me from myself and from all the injuries I may do myself while trying to be a blessing to others. Fill me with Thy power by the Holy Spirit, and I will go in Thy strength and tell of Thy righteousness, even thine only. I will spread abroad the message of redeeming love while my normal powers endure.

Then, dear Lord, when I am old and weary and too tired to go on, have a place ready for me above, and make me to be numbered with Thy saints in glory everlasting. *Amen.* AMEN.

A. W. Tozer
Reprint from *The Alliance Witness*
Quoted by permission of *Christian Publications*

Chapter 5

The Promise Is to You!

In the explosive atmosphere of Acts 2, this promise looks exciting! It seems to suggest that all that happened in the Upper Room and then the miracle at the Gate Beautiful is open for us also, even us so very "far off" from New Testament days. I do not doubt for a moment that this is all possible. God never intended His church to backslide. He never suggested, at least to my understanding, that apostolic power and blessing would be withdrawn before the coming of the King.

The trouble, as I see it, with the *present* interpretation of "the promise to you" is that:

> It is all sugar and no salt,
> all daylight and no darkness,
> all pleasure and no prisons,
> all privileges and no privations,
> all feastings and no fastings.

While I do not believe that there is a living soul who can scripturally prove that the gift of tongues is the "evidence" of the baptism in the Holy Ghost, let me say with equal emphasis, I do not believe there is a living soul who can scripturally prove that this gift or any of the others have been withdrawn. And yet the promise was not "ye shall receive tongues after that the Holy Ghost is come upon you." It was that "ye shall receive power."

The promise was not "ye shall always *hear* a sound of a rushing, mighty wind"; nor again, "ye shall always *see* a tongue of fire sitting upon each head." The promise was "power"!

Right here I'm thinking again of that smart word of Charles H. Spurgeon's, "The Bible suffers more from its exponents than from its opponents."

From the Upper Room the Spirit-endued believers were not taking a banquet and breakfast route to celebrate with celebrities the wondrous works of God; they were heading for persecution, for punishments, for prisons, for privations. These men needed power to heal the sick and they did not need the comfort of a super building to do it in. Neither did they need massive love offerings, or clapping, awed admirers to get them to operate. They saw sickness as a sign of the curse, and He who bore this curse in His own body on the tree told them to liberate the captives, undo heavy burdens, and let the oppressed go free—for *free*! "Freely ye have received, freely give." The ONLY right a preacher has to ask for offerings for his ministry is to pay back to GOD what God charged him for that ministry (charlatans exit here!).

These apostolic men needed power—to raise the dead! If a man falls from the gallery due to the long sermon and dies from his fall, the preacher had better have this power also. These men needed power, spiritual power, to announce the risen Lord against the monopoly of Jewish religion and the hatred of the crowd that crucified the Lord of glory. However mystified the crowd was with the speaking of tongues, they were not in any doubt about the message these burn-

ing men preached in their burning speech. The once stam-
mering tongue of Peter denying his Lord is now sharpened
by the Spirit until it hacks like a two-edged sword into the
minds and consciences of his hearers. Now the fearless,
fiery tongues of the Apostles burn eternal truths into hearts
once rock-like and immovable.

"Ye shall receive power" must have included mental
(they were to write epistles) power also. The Apostles were
to be hauled before magistrates and openly scorned as "unlearned and ignorant men." That is a sharp arrow to tear at
the pride of the "great" preachers. They needed mental
power to stand the constant snubbing by the ecclesiastical
elite who had cornered the market for sacrificial rams and
other essential offerings for the dead ritual of the day.
These men had no priestly clothing. (Can you imagine
them strutting like present-day evangelists with their alligator shoes, double knits, and "styled hair"?)

The apostolic preachers were the mavericks of their day,
or labeled as iconoclasts. They were eloquent by what they
did not say about the new moons and sabbaths. They were
effective by their total indifference to the temple sacrifices.
They were effective without showmanship, without human
patronage, without "healing meetings" and big offerings.

"Ye shall receive power" covered all their needs. They
had received a divine commission. God's callings are His
enablings. His promises are His provisions. He may reduce
Gideon's strength in the flesh and make "a fool" out of men
marching day after day before capturing the city. But remember, those men had one clear proof that they would
win; they had with them the ark of His presence. Is there
anything that can stand against His presence? Tucked deep
into the hearts of these staunch Apostles was the promise,
"LO, I AM WITH YOU ALWAYS." Could there be any-

thing more than this? Would anything less do then or now? In his massive epistle to the Romans, Paul says in chapter 8, "The Spirit . . . shall quicken your mortal bodies." The Apostles needed physical power also. We claim this for headaches—they claimed it for battered bodies, whip-lashed flesh, and lacerated limbs. They needed the inner fortification of the Spirit to out-match the tribulations of the flesh. Christ—risen, exalted, and indwelling them—was their sufficiency.

Words, words—millions of them—are trotted out every Sabbath day by preachers "in defense of the gospel." But Paul said, "My gospel was not in word only, but in demonstrations of the *Spirit* and of *power*."

Much has been said and written about the power of Acts 1:8 as power to testify. It was more than this. The word power there is *dunamis*, translated eight times in the New Testament as "miracle." But what miracles did the Apostles do *after* Pentecost that they did not do before the Upper Room enduement? They healed the sick and in jubilation and excitement told their Master, "Even devils are subject unto us." *Dunamis* is translated seventy-seven times in the New Testament as "power." These men received this power, the world knew they had it, and hell shook because they feared nothing and nobody, for God had not given them the spirit of fear, but of love and of power and of a sound mind. This power to them meant power to be martyrs!

This power was not sought as a cloak, for this would leave old king "self" in the middle still. But the Spirit of the Lord clothed *himself* with Gideon. God-centered men are the need of this hour, not men who want power to strut, nor power to call the world's attention to their "great" ministries. We need God-endued men whom hell fears. Our great need in this new century for America is a restoration *of apostolic power, apostolic purity, and apostolic piety.*

Today on a vast television show, a man can be telling the world he is Spirit-filled, and a few nights after be on the same vast network fooling with the fleshpot crowd. What an abomination! Oh for men clothed with and controlled by holy power! Paul is a good example. Let him speak for himself. Here is his record from 1 Corinthians 9:

Verse 4: "Have we not *power* to eat and to drink?" He had *power* over his appetites, the right to accept or to reject food sustenance (v. 27).

Verse 5: *"Power* to lead about a sister?" *Power* over his emotions. The right of an Apostle to marry or to be single.

Verse 6: *"Power* to forbear working?" Power to overcome the slander of the Greeks and others that manual labor was undignified and below the standing of an intellectual.

Verse 12: "We have not used this *power.*" He had not exploited the folk with whom he labored.

Verse 18: "I abuse not my *power* in the gospel." He had no price tags on his ministry. He had not sullied the Holy name of the One who called him by mercenary interests. Our radio preacher-beggars might read this chapter at leisure!

The glamor shows of today's evangelism over the television circuits has everything that savors of Hollywood and slick Madison Avenue methods. It lacks one thing supremely—power! The divine *dunamis! I would like to see a national day of repentance for evangelists.* Let the big boys take the lead and the lesser lights follow. Let US humble ourselves under the mighty hand of God, acknowledging our pride in statistics, etc., and declare our power-bankruptcy which is so obvious.

Our present faded efforts to "reach the lost" are pitiable, something like trying to melt a massive iceberg by holding lighted matches to it. The free nations are slowly but relentlessly being hedged in by Communist powers. The mass of people are sick over the political inertia of the hour. We, the pew dwellers, have been told for the last twenty-five years that world conferences on revival would usher in a new day. But here we are, powerless and ignored by a perishing world. WE need the *dunamis*. Maybe, nay, surely we need ten days in an Upper Room or maybe more suitable for us a basement to mourn the departed glory, to apologize for our arrogance in preaching so long without a NATIONAL revival.

Famed Finney said he had repeated baptisms of the Spirit; William Booth of the Salvation Army got a clean heart; George Fox of the Quakers found an experience in God that kept him sweet in all circumstances.

"The promise is to YOU!" Have YOU received this power? Read Acts 2 on your knees!

Chapter 6

The Last Days

These are the last days. The question is, how long will they last? A man with his finger on the pulse of the sick Church has this to say, "The Church in our generation needs reformation, revival, and constructive revolution . . . . Reformation refers to a restoration to pure doctrine; revival refers to a restoration in the Christian's life. Reformation speaks of a return to the teachings of Scripture; revival speaks of a life brought into its proper relationship to the Holy Spirit. . . . There cannot be true revival unless there has been reformation; and reformation is not complete without revival. Such a combination of reformation and revival would be revolutionary in our day." So says Dr. Francis Schaeffer in his book, *Death In The City*. This brought to mind some words my late dear friend, Dr. Tozer, spoke to me in his office one day. "Len, true revival alters the moral climate of a community." Does it do this in our church revivals? In this sad hour in our Nation's history, the optimists have gloom and the pessimists have doom.

Never in history has this great Nation been so humiliated in the eyes of the world.

Remember with concern the symptoms predating collapse of the mighty Roman Empire. In his classic study of that mighty military machine, Edward Gibbon cites five primary causes for the dissolution of that great society:

1. The rapid increase in divorce and the undermining of the sanctity of the home.

2. The spiralling rise of taxes and extravagant spending.

3. The mounting craze for pleasure and the brutalization of sports!

4. The building of gigantic armaments and the failure to realize that *the real enemy* lay within the gates of the empire, in the moral decay of its people.

5. The decay of religion and the fading of faith into a mere form, leaving the people without a guide.

Are these five fingers of death gripping the throat of America (or England) today?

Powerful prophets are needed in this moment of history to move among the pigmy politicians.

The Arabs have us by the throat financially. The Russians plot behind our backs. We plan our own economic destruction by inferior workmanship in our products and at the same time demand higher wages. This great United States a few years ago produced 75 percent of the world's automobiles. Today we manufacture only 30 percent. We held dominion in the area of ship building. We have lost that monopoly also. We were the world's greatest nation in armaments. We take second place now.

The shocking display of nudity plus legalized abortion and protected homosexuality are grave symptoms of the decline and near fall of the Nation.

These *are* the last days. I wonder how long they will last. How long does God wink at the sin of a nation? How long do we pervert justice, oppress the poor and trample the Ten

Commandments—His perpetual moral laws—into the dust?

But when you have listed what you think is the last threat against this Nation, when you have counted the last armed man in the enemies' army, the last bomb he has stashed away to blast us, the last atom bomb to burn us and the last economic trick to break us, I will reply that if you think these are the main dangers to this once great Nation, you have missed it by a million miles.

The greatest threat to America today is not Communism, nor the Arab oil blackmail pressed upon us, nor the severe ecology crisis. The greatest single threat to America today is GOD.

God was married to Israel. He divorced Israel and has not bothered with her for 2000 years. Why does He have to tolerate our sin? Can He not walk out on us?

America has passed her 200th anniversary. We have been reminded that the Golden Age of great empires is 200 years. The decline of these empires goes like this:

> From bondage to faith, from faith to courage
> from courage to liberty, from liberty to abundance
> from abundance to selfishness, from selfishness to complacency
> from complacency to apathy, from apathy to dependence
> from dependence to bondage.

At what stage do you think we are in our present national life? It is my opinion that we have had our seven years of plenty—our fat years; and the seven years of want—the lean years—are here now. The life's "blood" of a modern mechanized nation is oil, and well the Arabs know this. There may be other powers behind them that neither they nor we know of at the moment. But is the real energy crisis a matter of economics or politics? Could it be that the only way to halt the sin of the Nation is to grind our billion wheels to a screeching halt? Sunday has become fun day. All the big ball games are on Sundays. The beaches are crowded—the family gets together there now. I am sick at heart when I read that the Castro despots in Cuba claim they have no prostitution or floor shows in their midst. China says that she has not one case of prostitution in ten million folk and no venereal disease. While these godless souls trumpet their virtues, I read that here in "Christian" America prostitution has been legalized in parts of Nevada, and I remember that abortion kills its helpless babes in the wombs. "Christian" England (in the past tense) has legalized homosexuality. All that is nude and lewd and crude gets high TV ratings. But when we have raked over the whole muck heap of this decaying civilization, *my greatest grief is to see a sick Church in a dying world*.

After the four hundred years of silence and suffering between the Testaments, after the death of morality in England, God raised up a prophet—John Baptist to prepare the way of the Lord, John Wesley to prepare the way of revival.

The garments of the high priest in the Old Testament are called garments of glory and of beauty. After seeing the high priest so richly panoplied, the sight of John Baptist must have been shocking! This bearded eccentric in his chronic austerity and with his vulgar tongue must have been shattering to the sleepy ritualists of the day. "You generation of vipers" is hardly theological or priestly language. This incandescent man shattered the silence of four hundred years. He was a voice crying in the wilderness, but his voice echoed in the throne room of the king.

This uncompromising, unusual, unpredictable sun-scorched Son-exalting messenger cleared the way of the Lord by laying the axe at the root of the tree. He was fearless in his fearful exposure of sin.

John Baptist had his leather girdle, George Whitefield had his leather lungs, George Fox had his leather breeches. The prophet for this day denouncing sin in places high and low may need a fiberglass suit with lungs to match to awaken this dull generation. Remember that John Baptist stepped into a totalitarian world, highly sophisticated, arrogant, and with a massive slave system. John could have lived longer had he bit his tongue instead of making others bite theirs.

He could have died a hero instead of a martyr had he opposed the slavery of the Roman Empire, had he merely denounced the cults of the day, had he just pled for the oppressed and gathered funds for the blind and lepers begging along the highway. He could have fought for the civil rights of those commanded to carry the baggage of the lordly Romans. He could have taken folk on tours to see the place where Moses divided the Red Sea, or to the national shrine where Elijah bearded the prophets of Baal. He might have sold "a piece of the rock" from which Moses got the Tables of Stone. He might have asked for the gift of healing. But, no, none of these. This holy man—filled with the Holy Ghost from his mother's womb—burned with a fire that earth seldom sees; he spoke with an authority that earth seldom hears; he ignored social privileges with a contempt that few men have had for place, prestige, position, and possessions. He, like Paul, could say, "This ONE thing I do." This man knew his time was short. (We must know this, too.)

This man was hurt because God was hurt by the nation's sin. John Baptist was no soothsayer, no smooth sayer of pleasant things. He knew what we seem to have forgotten—that God is of holier eyes than to behold iniquity.

Thank God for all that the last twenty-five years have shown us in evangelism—if it was the real thing. But when the general practitioner cannot solve the patient's sickness, the specialist is brought in. When the evangelists have failed; when the million-dollar crusade leaves little in its wake; when the TV evangelistic show is over; when the Bible schools hang their heads and say, "It is not in us"; when the theologians hide their blushing heads and swing the other way in their swivel chairs; when the seminaries say, "We have heard of the fame of revival with our ears, but we have no formula for it"; when all these helpless ministries fail and the Nation speeds its way to hell; while Rome and the Communists are marching on, while the Church is looking on—let the righteous cry, and the Lord says He will hear them. Let the house of God become a place of weeping for the glory of the Lord that has departed, and let His anointed cry day and night, "Send us our prophets, O Lord. Let this be the sign that in wrath Thou dost remember mercy."

We must fall before Him and be broken to pieces, or we shall fall before Him when He breaks us to pieces.

Chapter 7

The Countdown to His Coming

"The King Is Coming." With these Christ-honoring words the telecast of the James Robison crusade opens the way for the evangelist to reach the tens of thousands of listeners. The telecast closes with the same emphasis. I rejoice in this.

World War I ended with the signing of the Armistice at eleven o'clock in the morning, on the eleventh day of the eleventh month, eleven months from the signing of the Armistice with Turkey and eleven months from the time that General Allenby walked bare-headed into Jerusalem. Was God trying to tell the sleepy Church and a lost world that we were entering the twelfth hour in human history?

Despite the efforts of the now defunct League of Nations and in spite of the strivings of the crippled United Nations and with the blood of countless millions crying from the battlefields of the world, we are further from international peace now than at any point in history.

One sign of the end of this age is "wars and rumors of wars." But! The Prince of Peace is coming! How do I know? Here's why. *Jesus said*, "I will come again and receive you unto myself." *The angels said* to the disciples who saw Jesus ascending to heaven, "This same Jesus shall so come in like manner as ye have seen him go." *Paul said*, "The

Lord himself shall descend from heaven with a shout." I believe that the countdown for His coming started when the Jews won the Six Day War. Less than three million Jews pitched a battle against more than thirty million Arabs and licked them! At that time when the Jews went to the Wailing Wall to pray, they ushered in a new chapter in world history. Jesus had said Jerusalem shall be trodden down of the Gentiles, until the times of the Gentiles be fulfilled (Luke 21:24).

For the first time in 2500 years, the Jews were in full possession of their land. Moshe Dayan said that they will never let it go again. Compared with the world population, only a few people expected Christ's first coming. So it is now. The Christians expecting His appearing are few against the millions of unbelievers in the world.

The first time He came, He entered by a woman's womb. And *no one* saw Him enter.

The next time He comes, "every eye shall see him"!

The first time He came as a Lamb.

The next time He is coming as the Lion of the tribe of Judah.

The first time He came to redeem.
The next time He is coming to reign.

The first time He came to die.
The next time He is going to raise the dead!

The first time men asked, "Where is he that is born king of the Jews?"

The next time He is coming as the King of kings!

The first time He got a crown of thorns.
The next time He will get a crown of glory and of gold (Rev. 14:14).

The first time He came in poverty, to a stable.
The next time He is coming in power.

The first time He had an escort of angels.

The next time "he cometh with ten thousand of his saints."

The first time He came in meekness.

The next time He is coming in majesty!

I never fail to get moved to tears when a congregation sings what Matthew Bridges wrote almost a century and a half ago, "Crown Him with Many Crowns," or the majestic song of Bill Gaither, "The King Is Coming."

The *out*look on the world just now is exceedingly dark. But! the *up*look is exceedingly glorious—the King IS coming!

These are the incentives for His coming:

To witness, "The Gospel must first be preached to all nations."

To sacrifice, "My reward is with me" (Rev. 22:12).

To patience, "Be patient therefore, brethren, unto the coming of the Lord."

To prayer, "Watch and pray."

To holiness of life, "He that hath this hope in him purifieth himself."

I have been in some dirty cities and some dirty countries and seen some dirty people—civilized and among pagan tribes. But *I have never seen a dirty bride*! Will His bride be dirty? Could the Lord come right now with the Church impure with carnality? *"The bride hath made herself ready"* (Rev. 19:7).

We need a mighty cleansing revival in the Church to prepare the way of the Lord.

"He which testifieth these things saith, Surely I come quickly."

Are *you* ready for His coming?

The *King is coming*! The Spirit and the Bride say COME!

Chapter 8

There Was a Man Sent from God

The people who had been to the temple that day and seen the high priest in his "garments of glory and of beauty" would find it difficult to accept this bearded eccentric of chronic austerity and vulgar tongue as "a prophet sent from God."

But Jesus said of this unusual, unpredictable, uncompromising man: "Among them that are born of women there hath not risen a greater than John the Baptist" (Matt. 11:11).

The secret of this amazing John Baptist is easy to discover. He was a single man, with a single eye to God's glory; a single purpose, to do God's will; and a single message to hail and introduce the Christ, the anointed of God, as the world's Redeemer.

Paul had the same single motive, "This *one* thing I do" (Phil. 1:13).

Men once separated to the gospel have become entangled again with the yoke of bondage through commercial interests.

John the Baptist had options also. He could have backed off from the dangers of a political and religious web of opposition, but the sun-tanned recluse accepted no social invitations, scorned political adoption, signed no contract to smooth the ruffled feathers of offended members of the synagogue. John the Baptist could have caused a nostalgic stir by preaching his message "on the very spot where Abraham, their father, offered Isaac!"

He could have taken tours to the place where fire fell after Elijah's prayer. He could have offered the many tourists a "piece of the rock" from which Moses got the stone for the Ten Commandments. He might have made a pile by showing the folk where Moses parted the Red Sea.

To get immediate attention, he could have blasted the Roman occupation of the country, or bitingly denounced the money-changing sharks in the Temple. He could have taken care of the social security of the blind and lepers on the wayside, begging. He did none of these things. Any of these mercy acts might have lengthened his ministry and his life. He did wrong in the eyes of the upper scions of society by preaching righteousness!

Predictably, the listeners were suspicious of his message of a coming King. Kings were not in favor—look at Caesar! But when his trumpet voice shattered their soul sleep, stirred their minds, and awakened their consciences, they were interested.

The new King, said this fearless man in the presence of foreign soldiers, priests, and populace, and an atmosphere thick with dissent, would overthrow the existing state of things. The new hermit cried, "Every valley shall be exalted." This surely was poetic language, meaning the downtrodden would be lifted up. "Every mountain and hill made low" could mean none other than thrones overthrown, oppressors scattered, and lesser rulers unfrocked. Had the sun-tanned recluse stopped there, he might have gotten acceptance. But he became an offense. Which prophet didn't?

The Baptist said, "Now the axe is laid unto the root of the trees: therefore every tree which bringeth not forth good fruit is hewn down, and cast into the fire" (Matt. 3:10). Unless this strange man could raise an army, he could not smash the iron feet of Rome or unseat the materialistic, politically minded priests. But, John's attack was not against an effect but against a cause—sin. He was not troubled at that moment with a people who were hurt, but with a God who was suffering that His laws were broken, His Sabbath defiled, His house made desolate.

This undisturbed prophet disturbed everyone else. He did not attack slavery, though some scholars have estimated that there were some six million slaves in the Roman Empire. He did not attack the cults of the day (except when they came to him). The sect called the Essenes, who had fled Jerusalem and established a community not far from John in the wilderness and specialized in prophecy, were ignored, though they esteemed themselves the proprietors of "the whole truth" in that day.

John, as a prophet, was a success by any measure of standard. Socially he reached all classes—all were sick of unrighteousness, injustice and oppression.

Like flames on a burning building at midnight, this desert-bred prophet attracted the soldiers, foreign legions, the people, and the publicans. He spoke a language they had not heard, but they understood it. He spoke the truth, a thing lost in that day and in this also.

John attacked no social diseases, no war policies. His message was righteousness. He attacked sin. He said it would ruin men as individuals, destroy communities, and shatter nations, adding that righteousness exalteth a nation.

John had no easy believism. He did not offer a smiling penitent "pie in the sky, nor a mansion over the hilltop and a crown of glory, plus a free ticket to the Marriage Supper of the Lamb, and a perpetual reward of rulership over five cities"—all for a two-minute apology to God, plus a baptism ritual.

There is much talk today about the gifts of the Spirit, and they are beautiful when genuine; less talk of the fruits of the Spirit; still less emphasis of "bring forth therefore fruits meet for repentance" (Matt. 3:8).

The modern evangelist, usually a cheerful fellow, offering free pardons for mighty offenses against a holy, righteous God, offers too much for too little. Now we shall be charged by the unknowing, with demanding works for salvation. Well, if repentance preaching is offering works, lay the charge at John the Baptist's feet, lay it on Jesus (Luke 5:32), lay it against Peter for his Pentecost sermon.

There are as many types of preaching as there are types of preachers. Some preaching is edifying but not convicting. Some is directed to the emotions, some to the intellect. That of Jesus, John the Baptist and Peter attacked the conscience as well as the will. These three had one thing in common: the anointing of the Holy Spirit.

Before His ministry, Jesus was anointed of the Spirit and declared it: "The Spirit of the Lord is upon me, because he hath anointed me—to preach" (Luke 4:18). They were all filled with the Holy Ghost—and Peter stood up, lifted up his voice. It was said of John the Baptist what was not said of any other man that ever lived, "He was filled with the Holy Ghost from his mother's womb" (Luke 1:15).

Our present-day effete evangelism with its emphasis on happiness would have shocked John the Baptist. We try to induce happiness on a heart diseased with sin. We offer

Band-Aids to folk who need radical spiritual surgery for the cancer of carnality in the breast.

We preach to produce peace in the heart. John the Baptist preached to produce panic! I hear preachers boast that after they finished preaching, men of the congregation carried them shoulder-high around the auditorium. That's a sure sign that the preacher and his preaching missed the mark.

Heathen soldiers heard John the Baptist and found that their breastplates of shining armor could not keep the arrows, fire-tipped with God's judgment, from entering their hearts. Altar calls are a modern convenience to get results when the Holy Ghost has not honored the truth. Look at this picture: Spirit-anointed John the Baptist, preparing the way of the Lord, scorches all hearts as he preaches a Word quick and powerful and sharper than any two-edged sword.

The afflicted soldiers made the "altar call." They cried, "What shall *we* do?" (Luke 3:14). Having severed their blood-line to Abraham as invalid for either mercy or forgiveness, the people cried to John the Baptist, "What shall *we* do?" (Luke 3:10).

The covetous, conscienceless publicans withered under John the Baptist's soul attack, and they, too, cried, "What shall *we* do?" (Luke 3:12).

The men who preach our revivals (!) are evangelists, not revivalists. Revival shatters the status quo. We can no more have a Spirit-born revival without a moral and spiritual upheavel than we can have an earthquake without destruction.

With all our know-how and technical advances in agriculture, men still do not gather grapes from thorns or figs from thistles. Neither do we get Holy Ghost revivals "over the air" or by staging mass crusades. Babies are born only after travail (Isa. 66:8). Revivals are birthed by spiritual giants, not slick talkers and golfing evangelists. Let history teach a few lessons right now.

When a woman said to George Whitefield, "Sir, I have listened to you preach five times in three days and each time I have been wetted with your tears," she was revealing that the great soul winner had himself wept for lost men in the secret place.

Remember, will you, that in a day without mass communications, the only way to reach a meeting was on foot, or by carriage which few could afford, or on a horse.

Yet when the population of Boston, Massachusetts, was only 12,000, Whitefield drew 14,000 a night to hear him. There were no black-top roads, no restaurants, no motels; buses were not known, trains were not there. Yet, such was the magnetism of a Spirit-filled man that the crowds listened and were moved of the Lord.

The plain but unusual preacher, John Smith, followed on the heels of Wesley. He says, "I am looking for deeper baptisms of the Holy Ghost." He urges another minister, "Get deeper baptisms," and adds, "If we were always filled with the Holy Ghost before we got to the house of God, we should see signs and wonders."

Tears for the lost were the daily exercise of these revivalists. The mighty Jeremiah said, "If ye will not hear it, my soul shall weep in secret places for your pride; and mine eyes shall weep sore, and run down with tears" (Jer. 13:17). The Prince of all preachers wept over Jerusalem (Luke 19:41). Arthur Fawcett says, " . . . the prophet is a manifestation of God's activity." History demonstrates this opinion.

An experience of God that costs nothing is worth nothing and does nothing. *I am convinced that the reason we do not have earth-shaking revivals like old times is that we are content to live without them!* Or, aware from the histories of these saints, that, while evangelism can be started and finished at the whim of men, revival can only be at the greatest cost—tears, travail, and the mercy of a sovereign God.

David Brainerd, greatly influenced for God through the mighty preaching of Jonathan Edwards, was ejected from the university for participating in revival meetings conducted by Gilbert Tennant.

November 25, 1742, Brainerd set off on his historic commission from the Holy One of Israel to evangelize the Indians. Five years later, wracked with tuberculosis in body and fevered greatly, he died and was laid to rest, accepted as a living sacrifice by the One who himself sacrificed himself for many.

Wesley took to the fields to preach as the doors of the churches and the denunciations of the bishops barred him from the pulpits. Of six hundred sermons he preached, only six of them were from the polished pulpits of the day. A rock became his podium, or even his father's tombstone. Evangelists get pampered and popular. Revivalists are penalized, ostracized, and lonely!

I am sure that we are ineffective preaching before men because we are impotent in pleading in prayer before God.

Tell me, with all the enthusiasm you have, about the shattering, soul-gripping preaching of Master Finney. I will reply with, "Yes, but remember that he had 'Father Nash' and 'Father Clary' holding him up in prayer twenty-four hours a day, like Aaron and Hur held up the hands of Moses." While Finney pled with men in public, Nash and Clary pled with the Lord in secret. Result? Revival!

When Saul and the soldiers of Israel feared and failed and fled before the mighty Goliath, David stood in the breach. He scorned the man who scorned the God of Israel. From his own stout heart, he heartened the king and others. Listen to his confidence as he speaks of Goliath, "Let no man's heart fail because of him!" (1 Sam. 17:32). We need a David in this hour of international tensions and trembling as the money markets fail and we face distress of nations with perplexities.

Like Israel, we have had our seven years of plenty, and now the famine comes. Fear not!

Here in the United States we live like kings compared to millions in other lands. Our greatest danger is not even moral, bad as that is, but spiritual. Prophets, as I have said and written so often, are God's emergency men for crisis hours. They thrive on perplexity, override adversity, defeat calamity, bring the new wine of the Kingdom to burst the withered wineskins of orthodoxy, and birth revival.

Let no Christian's heart fail him because it seems that the enemy has come in like a flood, that the voice of the prophet is not heard in the land. God has His men hidden. They will come forth without price tags; with nothing to sell, nothing to propagate but "holiness unto the Lord."

John the Baptist came at a critical hour in the history of Israel. The parched souls sought him in the heat-laden desert. Remember again the stirring and, I think, stinging words of Professor Harold B. Khun of Asbury Seminary, "Christianity was not served to the world on a silver platter; it was born into a sophisticated world with a totalitarian power over it."

England, dead under the teaching of Deism and thickly foul with corrupt politics, hardly offered loving arms of embrace to the Oxford scholar, Wesley. Slavery abounded and was legalized. England had a contract with South America to deliver her about 5000 slaves a year for thirty years. People were hanged for a slight damage to Westminster Bridge or for shooting a rabbit. Children as young as ten years were hanged for these offenses.

Injustice, unequal taxation, vice, drinking, etc., were all at a premium at Wesley's entree. In the latter years of the eighteenth century, England was "cursed with a lunatic king and a distracted regency," and later by a monarch, George the Fourth, who would have been less of a scandal to the nation if he had been a lunatic.

To the nation dead in politics and with icicles on the pulpits and snowmen in them, Wesley brought the torch of Holy Ghost anointed preaching and the nation melted before him.

The cultists and purveyors of false doctrines, with millions to spend on scattering their false doctrines worldwide, offer us greater challenges than Wesley or Finney had, but not greater than our God is able to deal with. Our present evangelism offers men a change of destiny; biblical regeneration offers men a new Spirit-born personality, then destiny.

The evangelism of the last twenty-five years has been the most costly in history. High-powered methods have needed high-powered men with high salaries to get them to function. Revival never costs a penny. It is the Lord's doing and is marvelous in our eyes.

Wet-eyed, heartbroken revivalists produced wet-eyed, heartbroken sinners at the feet of a holy God. "True revival," said dear Dr. Tozer, "changes the moral climate of a community." Men like John the Baptist burned their names on the history of the world.

I say again, the cost of getting near to the heart of God,

hearing the voice of God, and doing the will of God is great. God cannot be hurried. The back side of the desert—lonely, poor, uninviting, quiet—is the place where the bush burns, where the voice is heard, where the vision is given, where the marriage to His will takes place.

Evangelists come in teams. Prophets are always alone. From the school of prayer, from the desert place, men fired in the furnace of revelation and coveting only strength to do His perfect will emerge to upset nations and deliver the people. The school of the prophets is never overcrowded. There is no known curriculum. God shapes the man to suit the hour. One simple factor is obvious in them all: they are all lonely men, private men, passionate men, powerful men, persecuted men. They know that they have to bleed to bless.

At the moment, we are a broken nation, broken financially, morally, and spiritually. If we were half as spiritual as we think we are, we would be going to the house of the Lord in sackcloth with a handful of furnace ashes to anoint our unworthy heads.

But we still play church. We still delight in shallow preaching and offer shallower praying. Our sackcloth and ashes would be less conspicuous than Isaiah "walking naked and barefoot" (as a slave) for three years as a sign.

Jeremiah mourned the sin of the people. His castigations of their iniquity cost him a spell in the stocks, the inside of a prison, and the misery of sleeping at the bottom of a muddy well. He knew better than to say "peace, peace" when there was no peace. He alone knew the pending judgments of God. "I sat *alone* because of the wrath of God."

Oh, for men who will wait upon the Lord, hear His voice, get a baptism of His power and an authority to deliver His message to a sick Church and a dying world.

We have labored in the flesh too long. We have interpreted success by material gain—bigger buildings for our churches, bigger crowds for our hearers, bigger offerings, as proofs of His favor. We have had pygmy preachers too long. God, give us giants! We have had promoters too many. Lord, send us revivalists. We have played evangelism with a hundred gimmicks. Lord, give us, in this dark hour of human history, some John the Baptists to burn and shine, some Knox to say, "Give me Scotland [or England, or America], or I die."

> Revive Thy work, O Lord.
> Give Pentecostal showers.
> The glory shall be ALL Thine own.
> The blessing, Lord, be ours.

Theologians there are who insist that revival is a sovereign act of God, independent of human agency. This cannot be so. The whole stretch of human history since Pentecost is against this view. How is it that explorers never find a Christian community *unless* the missionary has been there?

If God works without men, then why did He tell the disciples to tarry until they be endued, then say, "Go ye"? The petty Peter of pre-Pentecost days became the prophet preacher of post-Pentecost days. Where is the heart-pricking preaching of this day?

Revival is the act of the Spirit upon believers who have lost their first love.

Revival is the restoration of true doctrine.

Revival is the rekindling of the power of prayer in individuals and in groups.

Revival is seeing that God must be vindicated either by His mercy in pardoning—or by judgment!

Revival is the ascendancy of the spiritual over the material.

Revival is the Spirit's passion within the believer to

know and to obey the total will of God.

Revival is the willingness to forsake all—that God might be all-in-all to the individual and to the Church.

Revival is the "no-time-limit" operation of God on the saints, resulting in a moving of God among the sinners.

Revival is the redeemed, sobbing with broken hearts over a nation of broken lives from breaking the commandments of God.

Revival is not a luxury, but a necessity for our Nation; not an alternative, but an imperative. Only a simple, unlearned evangelist would expect to break up the fallow ground, sow the seed, water it, and gather a harvest in twenty minutes.

I see *no* scriptural basis for a one-night meeting or a week's meetings. These are modern innovations. Paul never operated this way, neither did Finney. Revival means blood, sweat, and tears. When Zion travailed, she brought forth (Isa. 66:18). Object to this you may; but God wrote the rules; and when we obey, He operates. "Ye shall seek me, and find me, when ye shall search for me with *all* your heart" (Jer. 29:13).

Chapter 9

The Discipline of Truth

In this day of thin theology, gospel peddlers (I hardly dare call them evangelists) have accented *free* grace until some such teaching has become a *dis*grace.

Men will not always say in clear words what they imply in their teaching. But the average evangelist, with his eye on the crowd or on the love offering, has a "gospel" which, in Paul's words, is "another gospel." It goes something like this:

You have done wrong (the ugly word "sinned" is omitted), this will ruin your life (not, "sin will cast you into hell"); come and tell God you are sorry (not, "bring forth fruit therefore meet for repentance"). Now don't sob like that (though God says "a broken and a contrite heart"), the Lord understands; now that you have prayed, all is well. Just think of it this way: your name is now written in the Book of Life. You will have a mansion over the hilltop, a crown and free ticket to the Marriage Supper of the Lamb and will be made a ruler over five cities.

This, if it were true, would classify for the title, "The Great Give-Away."

More than ever I want to emphasize that when dealing with "seekers" we need to get them to "read the fine print."

One *guarantee* that is not so electrifying reads, "In the world ye *shall have tribulation*." This is a real part in discipleship. It seems strange to our tender ears, but Paul actually craved this! Listen to him: "That I may know him and the power of his resurrection *and the fellowship of his suffering*." Could it be he craved the tearing nails through *his* hands and *his* feet?

There is no evidence that Jesus was ever sick. There is none to prove that Paul ever was either. What then is the suffering that Paul wishes to share? Are we spiritually healthy if we, too, crave that suffering?

There are some who interpret the present emphasis on the "charismatic" in the church as being for those who seek a spiritual emphasis. "It gets folk out of boredom." "It shatters the old ecclesiastical ritualism," etc. I am not satisfied that this is true in total. But there is no question that—in most circles exercising the charismatic tenor— happiness, not holiness, is in the forefront of the fellowship teaching.

Can you imagine a "five dollars a plate dinner" or "breakfast" with people seeking "the fellowship of his suffering"? I cannot.

The title of this chapter is "The Discipline of Truth." Nothing is more shattering than Bible truth.

The cheap message of the popular evangelist will be exploded by testing it with the truth of the Word.

I was provoked to these thoughts by the scripture, "Him that *overcometh* will I grant to sit with me on my throne." This makes plain that this honored position is not for every believer, but specified as "to him that overcometh." The area of overcoming is not outlined here, but it is classified with "suffering." The obvious thing is that the overcoming is not what takes place in heaven, but the enthronement with Him is because we have been overcomers while in this mortal flesh. Let me say again, this to me means the discipline of truth. Get this clearly that we are in a combat area. This is enemy territory. There are ambushments. There are traitors around. There are pitfalls. There are convenient stretches of compromise on the road of life. Believers beware, "Hold fast to that which thou hast that no man"— notice, *not* "no demon," *not* "no circumstance," but "no man" with some seducing spirit or doctrine of devils— "take thy crown." As never before, we need to "try the spirits." To fall short of complete triumph in Christ is to hurt His cause and to slander His name. To run the race that is set before us we must strip ourselves of all excess baggage. By this self-appointed action, we shall have contempt for the worldly systems, contest from the flesh, and counteraction from the devil. Lest we get the jitters over the "opposition" of this trinity—the world, the flesh, and the devil— we must again be disciplined with truth.

First, that the Lord "hath not given us the spirit of fear; but of power, and of love, and of a sound mind."

Second, that our exalted Lord finished the work that the Father gave Him to do (John 17:4), which was to ransack the power of darkness. Paul puts it this way, "And having spoiled principalities and powers, he made a shew of them openly, triumphing over them in it."

Third, the Book says Christ "hath delivered us from the power of darkness and translated us into the kingdom of his dear Son." So we are already "in the kingdom." We should be reigning even now over every foe that previously held us in bondage.

The explanation for this overcoming life is:

1. Their covering (Rev. 12:11), "the blood of the Lamb,"
2. Their conviction, "the word of their testimony,"
3. Their covenant, "They loved not their lives unto the death."

The reward for this overcoming is:

1. Rev. 2:7, "to eat of the tree of life."
2. Rev. 2:11, "shall not be hurt of the second death."
3. Rev. 2:17, "to eat of the hidden manna."
4. Rev. 2:26, "to him will I give power over the nations."
5. Rev. 2:28, "I will give him the morning star."
6. Rev. 3:5, "the same shall be clothed in white raiment."
7. Rev. 3:12, "Him . . . will I make a pillar in the temple of my God.
8. Rev. 3:21, "To him that overcometh will I grant to sit with me in my throne." That's the ultimate reward and glory.

Link all this truth together and we are, if we obey it, disciplined for the day of His appearing, nerved for a holy walk in this present evil world, for "he that hath this hope in him purifieth himself."

For the Spirit-born, Spirit-controlled believer, the overcoming life is "The Normal Christian Life." Worthy is the Lamb who made all this possible.

Chapter 10

A Famine of Hearing the Word of God

The pushing, promoting, and promoted "personality" preacher is a phenomenon of our troubled day. I cannot think of Amos, of whom I am writing, or any other prophet, major or minor, needing an "Advance Man" to herald his coming, any more than I can think of him in double knits and alligator shoes with a dummy on his knee!

Woe unto us that the pulpit is now so anemic, so pathetically lacking in Holy Ghost magnetism that so-called intelligent people have to be reached on the children's level with a dummy to speak and a dummy to operate him! This is about as far removed from Pentecost as mud is from gold.

Prophets were known for their stern rebukes and tears, not for making religious wisecracks.

The newscasters are constantly reminding us of threatened famine. There is already a beef shortage, a grain shortage, a cattle food shortage, gas shortage, and now a threatened bread shortage. And all this not in a time of war, but a time of uneasy peace amidst a glut of production technology. Amazing!

Russia has trapped us again. She ran off with our grain, hence the shortage of feed for cattle, farm foul, etc., and the threat of a bread famine. She smiles about her recent agreement with Washington about cultural exchange. She has already shown her iron hand. *Jesus Christ Superstar* will not be allowed in Russia because it has a religious theme! (It should be banned everywhere!) That rejection does not matter; it's the fact that she is already dictating the policy that does.

There is a greater and much more important famine in the land right now. It is a famine of the hearing of the word of the Lord. It will not fill our cemeteries with bodies; it will fill hell with eternal souls.

This famine of spiritual bread is told us by Amos. He was a prophet. Men have listed him as a minor prophet, but he uttered major truths! The prophets were a rare breed of men. They were God's emergency men for crisis hours. We need them at *this* hour in the history of America.

The prophets were God's Cabinet Members. He whispered His secrets to them. They shared His foreknowledge. Amos himself declares this amazing fact to be so. Hear him from chapter 3, verse 7 of his prophecy: "Surely the Lord God will do nothing, but he revealeth his secret unto his servants the prophets."

But Amos comes with no swagger, he has nothing to promote, no cause to advertise, no organization to support, no funds to be raised. Amos is not usually called a prophet of fire, but eight times in the first two chapters of his book he mentions fire. His utterances are enormous, his predictions accurate, his warnings as fierce as they were unheeded. Yet in the first verse of his writings, he reminds us that he spoke these Spirit-born revelations "two years before the earthquake." This earthquake was mentioned by Zechariah (14:5) in the time of Uzziah. Amos was prophesying when Jeroboam was king of Israel and Uzziah king of Judah.

The records show that the later years of the reign of King Jeroboam were marked by great material prosperity. This is evidenced in chapters 3:15, 5:11, and 6:4-8. The wine-drenched merchants, languishing on their beds of ivory, challenged the discipline and destruction by the Lord God Jehovah. The folk who drew their wealth from the grinding of the poor fooled themselves that they were a privileged class favored by God. They forgot His laws, or ignored them.

Prophets differ from preachers. Preachers usually "make" sermons; prophets bring a message from the Lord. The prophet has no meticulous care about a sermon of homiletical perfection or of exigetical exactitude. His soul is aflame. He usually carries a death sentence and as such is a solemn soul. He does not scratch itching ears. He is out of step with the current preaching style. He usually shocks.

The name Amos has been interpreted as "carrier." He carried his message not only to Israel but also to Judah. Israel was riding a prosperity wave at the time of Amos' word. They were secure from outward foe and had inward supplies. But the lust of the flesh, the lust of the eyes, and the pride of life had taken over. Amos was sent from Jerusalem to Bethel, which was the seat of idolatry and the center of calf worship. For all their iniquity and transgressions, the Lord will send judgment.

A close reading of this eighth chapter will show comparisons with the day in which we live. Verse one seems pretty, "A basket of summer fruit." But with the inner eye the prophet sees that this says "fruit." This is not the work of a day, but the season is over! The harvest is past, the summer is ended, and we are not saved. The fruit can only rot from here out. So with the nation then, so with us now. Verse three talks of the songs of the temple turning into howlings.

I am forced to draw a conclusion here. We have the most weird things hitting our ears these days in the name of music.

Verses four and six speak of the oppression of the poor. Recently the television showed "A Harvest of Shame"—the poor "wet-backs" who slave in the fields of this great land. One woman, 28 years of age with fourteen children, earned a dollar one day picking a miserable crop of beans. Children under the legal age for work were earning less than two dollars. A few huts where these poor souls live had no toilet facilities at all.

God does not overlook this wretchedness. A pastor working with the migrant workers said, "We still have slavery in America. But whereas we used to own them, now we rent them!"

I think that we often overlook the word of Isaiah (58:7). It is a condition of revival. "Is it not to deal thy bread to the hungry, and that thou bring the poor that are cast out to thy house? when thou seest the naked, that thou cover him"; and verse 10, "If thou draw out thy soul *to the hungry*, and satisfy the *afflicted* soul. . . ."

The people in the day of Amos had a respect for the Sabbath, but they could not wait until the sun had gone down and the moon gotten out of the way so that they could again short-change the people and shrink their bread basket (v. 5).

This is a day of monopolies, a day of cartels and managed prices by the big operators, but God will not overlook this either. In the day of Amos and in this day, God must judge sin. There are worse judgments than plagues of locusts, or tornadoes, or fire, or sword. The worst plight of all is not that of a nation in captivity to a foreign power, but the nation from which God has turned away.

We have had a thousand times more light than those of the day of Amos. We have turned our Sundays into fun days. Our folk want a minimum of the Word and maximum amusement.

God has set His own value and claims on the Sabbath. Let this be proclaimed with *trumpet voice* from every pulpit in the land. Let it be a memory verse for the thousands of students in our Bible schools:

> If thou turn away thy foot from the sabbath, from doing thy pleasure on my holy day; and call the sabbath a delight, the holy of the Lord, honourable; and shalt honour him, not doing thine own ways, nor finding thine own pleasure, nor speaking thine own words: then shalt thou delight thyself in the Lord; and I will cause thee to ride upon the high places of the earth, and feed thee with the heritage of Jacob thy father: for the mouth of the Lord hath spoken it. (Isa 58:13-14).

This may be hard on the Christian athletes who pay lip service to the Lord and then swagger before the crowds Sunday afternoon in the ball parks.

Just a couple of days ago a fine preacher brother said to me, "We have no great preachers in the country anymore." I think I know what he meant: no outstanding man with a "thus saith the Lord," a man terrible in utterance under the anointing of the Spirit. We have gifted preachers, talented preachers, orator preachers, famous preachers, organizing preachers, but where, OH where, are the preachers *who startle the nation with prophetic utterance*? There is a famine of great preaching, a famine of strong expository preaching, a famine of conscience-stirring preaching, a famine of heartbreaking preaching, a famine of soul-tearing preaching, a famine of that preaching like our fathers knew which kept men awake all night lest they fall into hell. I repeat, "There is a famine of the word of the Lord."

There is a famine of sound gospel preaching. "Easy believism" is the result of easy preaching. We need some sound preaching on *repentance, restitution,* and *righteous living.*

We need a trumpet voice again to tell sluggish believers that God requires holiness of His people. *There is a famine of true holiness preaching.* An awakening voice must tell the pew-dwellers that theology is the queen of the sciences, that holiness is the crown on the head of this queen, that God is holy, His book is the Holy Bible, His dwelling is a habitation of holiness, the Spirit is the Holy Spirit. The greatest thing that God can do on earth is to take a sinful man out of this sinful world and make that man holy and put him back into that sinful world and keep him holy. A man can be born of the Spirit, filled with the Spirit, bear the fruit of the Spirit, and have gifts of the Spirit. *There is a famine of preaching on ETERNITY:* of preaching on the glories of heaven, and the eternal misery of hell.

There is a famine of preaching on our obligation to get the gospel to the lost millions of men. This generation of Christians *is* responsible for this generation of sinners hearing the gospel.

When the Jews rejected His beloved Son, God forsook them. For 2000 years He has not spoken to them. He has given them no prophets. Will He forsake us, too? Where are the prophets?

Hear the psalmist in His bitter lament, "Cause thy face to shine [upon us], and we shall be saved" (Ps. 80:3).

Hear him again in Psalm 7, "If he turn not, he will whet his sword; he hath bent his bow, and made it ready. He hath also prepared for him the instruments of death; he ordaineth his arrows against the persecutors" (vv. 12, 13).

"Covet earnestly the best gifts." "He gave some apostles, some *prophets*." Preacher friend, covet this gift. This hour of Laodician Christianity demands it.

In this critical hour of America's history, we have no prophets! Gospel entertainment is at an all-time high. All nights of prayer are the order when revival is on hand. All-night sings are the fashion when the people are in spiritual decline.

Oh, for an Elijah!

Chapter 11

Who Weeps Anymore?

The Church as we know it today seems a million miles from the New Testament church. That may be a great generalization, but I'll stand on it. There is a gulf between our average Christianity and the church of the New Testament that makes the Grand Canyon look like a cavity in someone's tooth.

What is it that is missing from our churches? To use an Old Testament term, it is the burden of the Lord. One of the tragedies of the hour is that the voice of the prophet is no longer heard in the land. Where is the lamenting for the lost? Isaiah was a man heavily burdened for his people and their sin. So was Jeremiah; his concern for the people caused him to weep day and night.

The last revival mentioned in the Old Testament is found in the book of the prophet Joel. He proclaimed a solemn feast and said, "Let the priests, the ministers of the Lord, weep between the porch and the altar." Well, let's face it, who weeps anymore?

We need a revival in the Church, but we make a big mistake in placing the burden for revival on the pew. As I read the Scripture, God puts it on the pulpit. We need preachers who are eternity-conscious, who come to the pulpit bowed with the sin of the world, yes, and perhaps the sin of the congregation. Instead, we have someone coming along saying, "Look, just kneel here for five minutes and this is what you'll get: your name in the Lamb's Book of Life, a mansion on Main Street, a five-decker crown, rule over five cities, and a free ticket to the Marriage Supper of the Lamb."

I yearn to hear a voice that declares God's judgment on the godlessness he sees around him. Where is the denominational leader who has the gospel boiling in his veins as Jeremiah did in chapter 20? Many of our preachers seem incapable of being volcanic. Many sermons have become religious entertainment and move no one to tears of repentance.

The true prophet of God is not concerned first of all about the nation, or even about the Church. He is concerned that God is insulted openly; that God's laws are broken; that God's Son is rejected, and this in a land that is seemingly saturated with the gospel. Yet every day millions of sins are committed; the name of Jesus is taken in vain a million times; and all the while the country is inundated with religious messages.

Remember, Sodom had no preachers; Sodom had no gospel broadcasters. America has over seven thousand radio stations and almost every one of them, at some time in the day, carries a gospel program. But how many listen to it? The lights are flashing in the world around us; our civilization is on the edge of disaster and only a heartbeat from judgment; but who is warning us?

When Alexander Maclaren was called to the pulpit of a great Baptist church in Manchester, England, he sat down with his deacons and said, "Gentlemen, there is one matter to settle before I take this position. Do you want my head or my feet? You can have one or the other, not both. I can run around doing this and that and drinking tea, if you wish me to; but don't expect me to bring you something that will shake this city." God does not call men into the pulpit to become Jacks-of-all-trades to run errands. He calls them to get on their faces before Him. Dr. Maclaren's deacons got the message; but who gets on his face before God today?

When I speak to preachers as I have done frequently in recent years, I tell them, "You have nothing to do biblically except to fulfill Acts 6 by giving yourselves continually to the ministry of the Word and to prayer." In writing to the Thessalonians the Apostle Paul said, "I am praying night and day." What was he praying for? Not for a lost world or for the overthrow of the Roman Empire. He said, "I am praying night and day that I may see your face and supply that which is lacking in your faith." They had faith but it was deficient. It is the pastor's task to supply that lack.

The burden of the Lord in the Old Testament was not for the Amalekites, Hittites, Perizzites or Jebusites; God's chief concern was Israel. In the same way not a single epistle in the New Testament was addressed to the lost; every letter was addressed to Christians. Dr. Orton Wiley points out that the Epistle to the Hebrews contains not one word for lost men and women. Why? Because only a church strong in faith, a revived church, can be used of God to reach the lost.

The sickness of the Church, I believe, is twofold. First, we have taught people to witness and to work but we have not taught them to worship. Chirstians will not take the time before God to see Him in glory and majesty and holiness. I know preachers who think nothing of taking three days for elk or duck hunting, but who do not care enough about human souls to get down and fast and pray and seek the face of God. I know deacons who begin to fidget if the Sunday service runs five minutes overtime because they want to hurry home to watch the Bucks play the Goats. How do they think they will stand it in eternity?

The second cause of the Church's sickness is that the prayer meeting has become almost obsolete. I have visited some of the famous churches of the world and have discovered a curious thing about the mid-week service. Two-thirds of the average "prayer meeting" (if it is held at all) is actually a Bible study. A prayer or two is added at the end, and that's it. Paul said that he travailed in prayer. Are we greater than Paul? He said, "I travail in birth." I don't believe a man has a right to preach on the text "You must be born again" unless he has first "travailed in birth" that people can be born again.

Some pastors tell me that theirs is a New Testament church. Let me describe a New Testament church from Acts 4: the people went to church every day; they prayed every day; they broke bread every day; they brought souls to the Lord every day. Every deacon in that New Testament church was separated and tested to see if he was full of faith and the Holy Spirit.

What, then, is the burden of the Lord for today? He is concerned for sinners who are rebels, who have their fist up against God. He is concerned for preachers, that they should preach His judgment. And He is concerned for His church, the bride for whom He is coming. People ask me sometimes, "Are these the last days?" and I tell them "no." I think we're in the last minutes of this dispensation, or maybe in the last seconds as God counts time.

And yet—if I could, I would like to call together thousands of preachers in different countries of the world to spend a week in prayer for renewal. I would like to see them given instruction in prayer; not seminars on prayer, mind you, but exhortation to pray. We would spend the whole week praying, with periodic breaks. I believe this could be a detergent in the life of the Church. It would be a cleansing process. We could go back to our churches and perhaps stave off judgment, and God would usher in the revival that must come. Before Jesus comes I am convinced that we will see a great, sweeping Pentecost that will out-Pentecost Pentecost. God will pour out His Spirit on all flesh, as Joel said. Our sons and daughters will prophesy. God will produce a race of spiritual giants for the last mighty ingathering. Today God has these leaders hidden, but in the great Day of the Lord He will bring them to light, and the last shall be first. I pray that day will come soon.

Preach the Word

Shall I, for fear of mortal man,
The Spirit's course in me restrain?
Or, undismayed, in deed and word
Be a true witness to my Lord

Awed by a mortal's frown, shall I
Conceal the Word of God most high?
How then before Thee shall I dare
To stand, or how Thine anger bear

Shall I, to soothe the unholy throng
Soften Thy truths, and smooth my tongue?
To gain earth's guilded toys, or flee
The Cross, endured my Lord, by Thee.

What then is he whose scorn I dread,
Whose wrath or hate makes me afraid?
A man! an heir of death, a slave
To sin! a bubble on the wave!

Yea! let men rage, since Thou wilt spread
Thy shadowing wings about my head;
Since in all pain Thy tender love
Will still my sure refreshment prove.

Give me Thy strength, O God of power;
Then let winds blow or tempests roar;
Thy faithful witness will I be;
'Tis fixed; I can do all through Thee.

—Charles Wesley

Chapter 12

Is There Any Word from the Lord?

We were warned that they would come, and come they have—not in old rags with moldy bread and evil smelling. This new breed of scoffer is not from over the fence but from inside the camp, even the fundamentalist camp. They come dressed in Brooks Brothers clothes, trailing their degrees, soft spoken and patronizing their weaker brethren. Their scorn is just as strong and their pity for what one of them calls "the prophecy addicts" is just as bitter as any foul-mouthed hater of the blessed gospel and glorious hope of our Lord's triumphant return to rule over the earth.

What these elegant scorners have forgotten is that the Apostle Peter had their number 2000 years ago. They are, in fact, *a part of prophecy!* Peter says it this way, " . . . there shall come in the last days scoffers" (2 Pet. 3:3). Here they are vocal and vicious.

I am supposed to agree that the present evil days are but a repetition of previous days of manifest evil. Not so. The current swollen tide of impurity and iniquity is without parallel in history.

The Master Prophet, Jesus himself, said, "Ye can discern the face of the sky; but can ye not discern the signs of the times?" (Matt. 16:3). He also said in Luke 17:26, "And as it was in the days of Noah, so shall it be also in the days of the Son of man." The days of Noah, we are told in Genesis 6:11, were like this: "The earth also was corrupt before God, and the earth was filled with violence." Was the earth, the whole earth, as corrupt then as now? Was there ever violence in the streets of Sodom as in our streets? Were schools danger areas then as they are now? Just recently a television report said this of a California school: A dropout came back to see his teacher. He stood by the classroom door and let the teacher go in and out of the classroom twice. The third time she tried to leave the room he stopped her, closed the door, held the teacher at knife point and demanded that she strip. She was terrified. She saw that this was the boy who had raped and murdered a 16-year-old pregnant girl, murdered an elderly man, and now was raping her. The lad stole her jewelry and defiled her. She has suffered much since. The television man interviewing this poor victim asked what had been done to the boy. She replied, "Nothing that I know of." So iniquity swaggers and does not hide its blushing head because it never blushes!

This is the day of arrogant iniquity. It struts and strides, it screams from the billboards, it flashes from the television tubes. In a day when crime and cruelty saturate the press and television news, the public thirsts for more; it devours television mayhem, murder, and sadomasochism. This is the day when all that is vile, vulgar, vicious, vain, and virtueless gets the headlines; and millions of dollars are invested to see that this tide of moral scum does not decrease. The barbarians were a mild bunch compared to us educated savages. It took brains to invent a method to barbecue a city, but the atom-splitters have managed it. It took "science," the god of this age, to birth a system that would defoliate trees and blast a nation into a million miseries. Can you wonder then that a disturbed writer says, "We are the cruelest, most ruthless species that has ever walked the earth"? (Anthony Storr in *Human Aggression*). Paul Tournier put it this way, "The dance of violence goes round endlessly." While a close watcher of human events said, "This world is a theater of the absurd." Murders and muggings, vice and venereal disease are an accepted way of life right now.

In the light of all these indisputable facts, I am supposed to mute my message, soften my sentences, suffer in silence, and cringe as a Christian; because, say the Christian defeatists, "It was all prophesied: in the last days perilous times shall come." So it is prophesied that this day should not overtake us unawares. But the other side of this coin of prophecy is this, "I will pour out of my Spirit upon all flesh . . . BEFORE the great and terrible day of the Lord." If it is true that greater is He that is in us than he that is in the world, and it is true; if it is true that the gates of hell shall not prevail against His church, and it is true; then what have we to fear?

The believers must make a last-ditch stand against this lax, loose, licentious, lustful age; for all that is lewd, crude, nude, and rude is a way of life. IF the "church" has anything to say, she had better wake up, stand up, speak up, or shut up. I hear faintly amidst this moral turpitude and tiredness a faint cry, "Is there any word from the Lord?" The world is war-sick, sin-sick, and heart-sick over political corruption and feebleness to combat massive international plots and schemes against the United States. In a day of effete evangelism, glamorized gospel "shows," and television preachers who are often dubbed "gluttons for gold," we need to put our own house in order; then, as cleansed vessels, go out with trumpet voice to tell the world to "turn or burn," to repent or rot, to concentrate on prayer for forgiveness before it finds itself praying in concentration camps.

How much longer will the holy God wink at our national iniquity? Some want us to believe that the United States is destined to rule the world, that she is the Bride of Christ, that we uphold the Kingdom with our fading dollars. Let's keep this in mind that God was once married, but He divorced His bride for her adultery. Then ponder this: He has watched that bride get kicked around the world, scattered and pealed for 2000 years—yet He has given her no prophets! His terrifying silence has not reduced her to humiliation and repentance. Now consider us as a nation. Sure we have been blest above all others with wealth in these days; yet we pay lip service to God, but our heart as a nation is far from Him. We have on our coins "In God We Trust," yet we kick His Book out of our schools; we have legalized prostitution in one state; we have massive divorce; we have world records in alcoholic victims, in drug-ruined young people, in venereal disease amongst teenagers; we have some 40,000 people a year killed on the roads, mainly through intoxication; our jails are packed; our Nation worshipping by the millions at the shrine of sports; our television is saturated with nonsense and villainy.

But where, oh, where, is the trumpet voice of the Church warning men to flee from the wrath to come? Sure there are millions of believers who say that they believe Jesus may come today, yet they live in carnality. They talk far more about the Rapture than about this picture of our mighty Saviour, the Christ of God. I spell this picture in capitals—it should be shouted from the housetops and pulpit tops also. Ponder it:

THE LORD JESUS SHALL BE REVEALED FROM

HEAVEN WITH HIS MIGHTY ANGELS, IN FLAMING
FIRE TAKING VENGEANCE ON THEM THAT
KNOW NOT GOD, AND THAT OBEY NOT THE GOS-
PEL OF OUR LORD JESUS CHRIST: WHO SHALL BE
PUNISHED WITH EVERLASTING DESTRUCTION
FROM THE PRESENCE OF THE LORD, AND FROM
THE GLORY OF HIS POWER; WHEN HE SHALL
COME TO BE GLORIFIED IN HIS SAINTS. (2 Thess.
1:7-10).

Again, I ask, how long will the Lord of Glory wink at our
individual and national sin? Let men ask, "Where is the
sign of His coming?" and then read J. B. Phillips transla-
tion of 2 Timothy 3:1-5. It provides the answer:

> But you must realize that in the last days the times will
> be full of danger. Men will become utterly self-centered,
> greedy for money, full of big words. They will be proud and
> contemptuous, without any regard for what their parents
> taught them. They will be utterly lacking in gratitude,
> purity and normal human affections. They will be men of
> unscrupulous speech and have no control of themselves.
> They will be passionate and unprincipled, treacherous,
> self-willed and conceited, loving all the time what gives
> them pleasure instead of loving God. They will maintain a
> facade of "religion," but their conduct will deny its validi-
> ty. You must keep clear of people like this.

The disparity between New Testament Christianity and
today's sick Church in a dying world is a sorry sight. That
the Church is sick few will dispute. "The church seems almost indistinguishable from any other organization in society. You can't tell the Christians from anyone else," so
says Danny Rydberg, editor of *The Wittenburg Door*. Billy
Melvin, Executive Director of the National Association of
Evangelicals, expresses his concern for the Church of today
this way, "My concern is the measure of infiltration by the
world into the church. We have been influenced far more

than we would like to admit. This infiltration has dulled our effectiveness, blurred our vision, and caused us to adopt worldly standards of success."

A century ago Andrew Bonar said, "I looked for the church and found it in the world. I looked for the world and found it in the church." Are things any better today? Some churches would be totally offended if they were called "worldly" even if they have bowling alleys built in them and massive sports programs. From the bulletins I get from some churches, they seem to be the great entertainment centers.

Before I complete this book, let me take you back to a momentous event in history. "Look for a tough wedge for a tough log," so said Publius Cyrus. Lord Fisher was a tough wedge, but he had been put out of office in 1914 even though he had predicted that war with Germany would begin that year and that Captain Jellicoe would become England's Nelson. Winston Churchill sent a telegram to Lord Fisher asking for audience with him. Fisher said "no," believing that Churchill had jockeyed Reginald McKenna out of office. Then McKenna telegraphed a message to Lord Fisher saying, "Grant Churchill this interview." Fisher said "O.K." Churchill told Fisher that he had secret information that the Germans would soon burst out into the Atlantic and start a war. Here was Lord Fisher's stern statement, "Churchill, you must do three things and do them all by telegram *before you leave this room*. First, you must mobilize the fleet. Next, you must buy the dreadnoughts we are building for Turkey. Finally, you must appoint Admiral Jellicoe Commander-in-Chief of the Grand Fleet." To do either of the first two was a serious breach of Cabinet discipline; to do the last was to offend a string of Admirals senior to Jellicoe. Churchill hesitated; Fisher insisted. "What does it matter," he said, "whom you offend? The fate of England depends on you. Does it matter if they shoot you, or hang you, or send you to the Tower of London, so long as England is saved?" Churchill did as Fisher advised. Maybe it was the greatest political act of a life filled with courageous acts and maybe one of the greatest acts of all statesmanship. Lord Fisher remarked afterwards, "You may not like Winston, but he has got the heart of a lion."

Now, preacher friend, I believe this is the hour for the lion-hearted preachers. Our pulpits have been filled too long with too many puppets instead of heaven-born, holy fire-filled prophets. If Churchill could risk his neck for a temporal kingdom, isn't it about time we cast off dull sloth and put on the "whole armor of God" and declare a Holy War of prayer and fasting against this avalanche of hell that has fallen on our generation? The official book on spirituality says that we wrestle not against flesh and blood. No bombs ever destroyed a demon—no fasting, intelligent prayer ever failed to.

Our national plague of iniquity is beyond the power of statesmen; indeed, there are none of them left; we just have politicians. Banks cannot help us here. The unspiritual intellectuals are out of this race, seeing that they themselves are deceived and know nothing of the powers of the world to come.

Who takes the Church seriously as a world power anymore? We are a relic. We are "supported by vested interests," scorners say. Many still urge us to pray for the recovery of the dollar as an essential to spreading the gospel. Not so. There was no dollar interest in the mighty New Testament-type revival which Mel Tari and others witnessed a decade ago in Indonesia. That was a divine invasion of a country, the power of the other world on this world. It was revival!—something that most of us have never seen. The road to revival shatters our conceit. It defies our organization. The Christian has no "holy city" to crawl to, no Mecca, no Rome. His only hope is another visit to the Cross, this time to get *on* it and be crucified with Christ; then a halt at the Upper Room for that apostolic enduement which money cannot buy, ordination cannot give, and what cannot be inherited by flesh and blood.

Revival—no denomination has a monopoly on it, neither can we birth it or stay its birth. It ignores our massive, costly crusades. It evades our weekly million dollar radio outreach by preachers. To be painfully honest, what we have preached for the last twenty-five years by the biggest budgets that the Church has ever known has not moved the Nation to God. Why continue a formula that has been so patently ineffective?

If we had a "pope" in Protestantism, I would appeal to him to close all pulpits, all Bible schools, all seminaries for a month (Most of us do not need more light, we need more obedience.)—a month of heart-searching, a month of doing what Joel says: sanctify a fast, call a solemn assembly, with the priests and ministers weeping between the altar and the doorposts; with prostrate preachers acknowledging their spiritual bankruptcy and lack of love for souls, for such the Holy Word says, "Howl, ye ministers of the altar: come, lie all night in sackcloth, ye ministers of my God" (Joel 1:13). This is God's formula for revival. Is He bound to honor anything less than this?

A BROKEN AND A CONTRITE HEART, O GOD, THOU WILT NOT DESPISE. "Give ear, O Shepherd of Israel, thou that leadest Joseph like a flock. Turn us again, O God, and cause thy face to shine; and we shall be saved" (Ps. 80:1, 3).

Chapter 13

The Malady

Henry F. Lyte was born in 1793, just two years after John Wesley died. He wrote almost a hundred hymns. The best known of these is without a doubt, *Abide with Me.* Two lines of this fine hymn have troubled me today:

The darkness deepens . . .
Change and decay in all around I see.

Just minutes ago I was reading from *The Golden Cow* by Dr. John White. I quote: "The night will grow darker. If we are appalled at all that is happening around us, we have only begun to see the unleashed furies of blackness. THE FINAL DARK AGES ARE BEGINNING" (emphasis mine), page 170.

Change is happening more rapidly than ever. We, that is all humanity, are on a collision course with God. And God never loses in a confrontation. Decay is accelerating at an enormous rate. Things previously done in a corner are now done publicly with a strut! Who would have thought, even ten years ago, that thousands of homosexuals (real name Sodomites) would walk with banners flying down the main streets of American cities all on the same day, claiming their rights? This is not just an American phenomenon. Here and in other countries these sex perverts are coming out of the woodwork. Just a week ago an established church, centuries old, asked that its leaders seriously consider accepting Sodomites for the office of priesthood, guaranteeing these men exercise "wholesome conduct." One wonders if words mean anything!

Professor Thomas Howard of Gordon College wrote, "All religions and tribes and all myths have known that there are taboos—all of them, that is, except Sodom, Rome in its decline, AND US." (Emphasis mine.)

As a nation we seem determined to make our bed in hell. We have set our course and are following straight on. Only the church of Christ, inspired by the Holy Spirit, can create a national revival strong enough to stop this impending suicide. To reach our present state of catastrophe we have gleefully sailed past the wreckage of brilliant civilizations. We have scorned the Law and the prophets. Intellectually we have relegated Jesus Christ, the only Son of God, to the level of depraved mortals, notwithstanding Buddha, Confucius, etc.

We have ignored history and the historians and have turned a deaf ear to a million sermons. Having closed our eyes we are unaware that nemesis is overtaking us for our recent war crimes. Thousands have smiled at the warnings of present prophets. David Wilkerson gave us *Racing Toward Judgment.* In return he was blasted by many of his friends and derided by theologians. Dr. James Kennedy has given us *America on the Brink.* Did we heed? In an hour-long broadcast by the BBC Aleksandr Solzhenitsyn shattered the flimsy talk of the politicians. Asked what he thought of this mighty verbal onslaught, Malcolm Muggeridge said, "Its impact is due to the fact that it is absolutely true. You see, what Solzhenitsyn has said is on an entirely different level from the comments made by world politicians and broadcast on television. His comments were made in the terms of truth; in terms of good and evil; in terms, ultimately, of the Christian faith."

The impact of this master of literary power and ex-Russian captive was greater than anything that had hit England for fifty years. Did the politicians there or here (for it was rebroadcast here) take heed? Solzhenitsyn says that he would not "be at all surprised at the imminent fall of the West." He does not believe a word that the Russians say. He has all the inside information of the world's greatest prison camp—Russia. We, however, turned him away from the White House.

Is this oil crunch another warning from God? Will He have to give the sun a month's vacation, dry up all the rivers and split the Nation from coast to coast with a mighty earthquake to get our attention? While we wonder *what* to eat half the world is wondering *when* it will eat. Millions live daily in the valley of the shadow of death while we live at ease resting our over-stuffed bodies on over-stuffed furniture.

There is violence on the streets, off the streets, and in the prisons. Yet this is but a small thing compared to the inner violence of the masses. The cry is still "We will not have this man to rule over us." Though statistics say that 75% of the people living in the U.S. are born again, the moral state of the Nation denies it. Certainly millions *say* Jesus is the Son of God, and yet He is not the Lord of their lives. An old Scot used to say to us, "If He is not Lord of all, He is not Lord at all."

Corruption on every level could not be so high if millions of us were biblically regenerate. Profession of faith in Christ there may be, but the salt has lost its savor and so we continue to rot morally. David Wilkerson is my next-door neighbor. I know something of his grief over the Nation. I have known it since we labored with him in his early days in New York City. He could write "The Vision" because he had a vision. He is no swivel chair theologian. He has trod the midnight pad of the prostitutes; he has rescued the perishing and cared for the dying. He has the pulse of the Nation. His present crusade is against the alarming rate of suicide among teenagers and young adults. They have drugs, autos, lurid entertainment and what passes for dancing. So why are they dried up? Why are they restless and frenzied? The devil is a cruel master! When young people of the present generation, here and in other countries, yield themselves body, soul and spirit to the wiles of the devil, Lucifer accepts them as a living sacrifice and returns evil for evil, consuming them on the altar of iniquity. We blame the kids for reading pornography. Do they print it? No! Adults invest millions of dollars to trap kids in sexual lust. Young people drink. Do they own the breweries? Kids smoke pot. Do they grow it? They sneak off to see 'dirty movies.' Do they make them? Young people take 'the pill.' Do they manufacture them? Many of the folks who make this witches brew are religious people. Many of the owners of breweries and whiskey distilleries are very religious folk. What a judgment they will have! Adults have set the pattern for a sinning life-style. Is it any wonder that the children follow in their steps? The Bible talks about parents who eat sour grapes and their children's teeth are set on edge.

Political lying is well known. We are told that there is a genuine oil shortage; however, the *New York Times* of November 1978 tells another story. *Spotlight* (June '79) quotes it this way: "A little-noticed story in *New York Times*, Nov. 1978 [remember the date], says the Government plans to 'stage fake energy emergencies around the country in the next three years as a drill to gauge state and federal preparedness. Throughout the exercises, no participant will have advanced knowledge of the details of the scenarios or of the mock emergencies to be used.' "

New York Times book critic Richard Dudman, commenting on the book *Sideshow* by William Shawcross, says, "It would be hard to write the recent history of Cambodia—ten tragic years of devastation, war, and turmoil, and now invasion by the hated Vietnamese—without going into the miscalculations and deliberate lies of Henry Kissinger and Richard M. Nixon." Should we wonder that the kids pass off their own lying as a petty thing?

I believe that there is an unprecedented spirit of lying and deception in the earth today. Not the least of these are the lying prophets. Having rejected the One who is the way, the truth and the life, the alternative is to fall for other gods. Heresy, like so many other things today, is a multimillion dollar business. Kids who "cannot accept the Bible because it speaks of an everlasting hell" trumpet the Hare Krishna junk which says that a person will have to spend forty thousand years in burning oil for eating *one* hamburger! Having rejected the Light, kids embrace Eastern religions and then they fall apart morally. Buddhism teaches that "there is no God to save, no soul to be saved, and no sin to be saved from." Well, that's easy street.

In the introduction to his book *Our Savage God,* R. C. Zaehner wrote about Charles Manson, the sinister figure responsible for the Sharon Tate murders which shocked the world in 1969. "What was so peculiarly horrifying about these murders was that neither Manson nor his youthful accomplices, most of whom came from middle-class homes, showed the slightest remorse for what they had done. How was this possible?" On the same page of his book he answers his own question by referring to two books on the Manson case, *The Family* by Ed Sanders and *Witness to Evil* by George Bishop. "Both books seemed to show that not only drugs launched Manson on his murderous career, but also an experience which he termed *'enlightenment'* as preached by the religions of Indian origin."

Some think it uncharitable to talk of all these cults as demon power. Let the simple soul who so talks read *Crazy for God* by Christopher Edwards and so see what tortures the Moony-ites suffer.

Spiritism, demonology and the cults are having a field day right now. I burn when I read a modern writer speaking of the "ever changing world now emptied of meaning." I am convinced that young people and older folk alike reach for Zen Buddhism and the other cults because they are afraid to face the facts of sin and the biblical revelation that to *reject* eternal life means to *accept* eternal death. They would rather go to their grave blindfolded with unbelief and downright opposition to the Christian revelation than quit sin and self-living and take Christ as the Master of their lives. They see Christ only as a Master demanding total obedience. Their minds crusted with 'learning' of the modern type and surfeited with creature comforts while they listen to today's loud, sensual music, they are not their own masters but already slaves of the old master, Satan.

Let me round off this sorry tale of our present moral calamities with two illustrations. First, a reminder that when Paul the apostle went down Main Street Athens 2000 years ago, his spirit was stirred within him. The Amplified New Testament says "his spirit was grieved and *roused to anger*

102

when he saw that the city was full of idols." (And it was a city of intellectuals.) Do we react in this way to the temples of the cultists that line our city streets whether it be the Mooney-ites pressing us for cash, the Hare Krishna groups, or the local Jehovah's Witnesses? We seem to take them all in stride. Our attitude to this whole gamut of iniquity and parade of lying spirits trapping souls for eternity seems to be "Eat, drink, and be merry, for tomorrow we shall be raptured!"

The following quotation is taken from one of David Wilkerson's books. Read it carefully, weep and pray. It may be that your own child is warped in this web of wickedness:

The Two-Billion-Dollar Slap in God's Face

Smut has mushroomed into a two-billion-dollar-a-year crime-infested industry. While the church and the courts retreat and sit around in fear, Mafia allies are waging a full-scale war on decency and righteousness. Porno now invades every segment of this corrupted society.

What have we come to in America when an admitted former prostitute, Xaviera Hollander, sells nine million books boasting about her immorality? When *Playboy* magazine displays a cover with scenes of women masturbating? When topless chauffeurs whisk tourists in black Cadillacs from fancy hotels to sleazy massage parlors? When male hustlers stand on street corners, pouncing on passersby just as in Sodom? When sex becomes humiliating, filthy, and violent? When slick, expensive porno magazines, subscribed to even by ministers, carry articles and scenes on "how to make love to animals"? When bookstands carry brazen magazines on bestiality and sex with children? When San Francisco, the dirt capital of America, cannot prosecute a single smut pusher since 1971? When an influential university like Brandeis honors men who publish and distribute bizarre smut? When one company can gross over half a million dollars a year marketing whips, chains, and bondage devices for homosexuals and sadists? When "Midnight Blue," a three-times-a-week cable program in New York City, can run pornographic films in our Nation's most populated city? When more and more cities now show X-rated movies on TV after midnight? When *Vogue* magazine can feature a twelve-page fashion spread showing a man beating up the model for gratification? When rape scenes are glorified and sado-masochists are allowed to roam the streets in search of victims?

"They are all adulterers; as a baker's oven is constantly aflame—except while he kneads the dough and waits for it to rise—so are these people constantly aflame with lust" (Hosea 7:4, TLB).

The American "Right" to Perversion

How can God delay His judgment on a nation that defends pornography as a "right"? Recently, liberal First Amendment defenders rushed to the defense of an X-rated film, *Sweet Movie*, that featured unspeakable filth and degradation.

No wonder Dr. White says, "I tell you that unless deep and widespread repentance comes, terrible tribulation will take place in the West." (*The Golden Cow*, p. 170)

In the last century William Booth 'saw' the down-trodden lower class of society in England—the tired masses dying prematurely in the sweat shops from wrong and long hours—and those who lived, nearly going blind from sewing shrouds for corpses. Booth determined to win the least, the lost, and the last. God gave a nation-wide revival.

Today folks are dressed better. But the streets are full of leprous, lost souls. I once told David Wilkerson that if every church did its job, there would be no need for Teen Challenge as a separate organization. "For the Son of man is come to seek and to save that which was lost."

Israel had the Law and the prophets. It had a tempestuous course in and out of slavery to other nations, but did it heed? Last of all God sent His own Son. The smart but wild host said, "This is the heir. Come let us kill him."

Preachers like to talk about the Triumphal Entry of Jesus into Jerusalem. Why not change the title to The Tearful Exit of Jesus. He said, "Your house is left unto you desolate." They have had no prophets since Christ. For 2000 years the people of God have been a football for almost any nation to kick around. Will God's patience with us last much longer? Are we going into captivity?

In this chapter I have tried to describe the malady afflicting our Nation. But what IS the remedy? "That wonderful Redemption—God's remedy for sin."

Let's consider it in the next chapter.

Chapter 14

The Remedy

The Bible is never wrong! God does not have to retract, revise, repair, or recall one word He has ever spoken. He says, "Righteousness exalteth a nation, but sin is a reproach to any people." We, however, seem to live by a more popular rendition: technology exalteth a nation and sin is fun for any people.

God has spoken to us in these last days by His Son. In the days of St. Paul scoffers refused to listen. Peter also endured harassment by the critics. The main issue was the promise of His coming. Well, today the great grandchildren of the scoffers are still very vocal. However, today they also wear clerical attire. Yet we *are* sure of this: We are nearly 2000 years nearer to His coming than the New Testament scoffers were!

The gates of hell will not prevail against the living Church the living, exalted Christ. "I will build my church." He can do it, He is doing it, and He will continue to do it. The only imperishable thing on this earth is the church of the living God. Stand up and cheer!

Isaac Watts gave us the grand hymn "When I Survey

the Wondrous Cross." He gave us this great hymn also, "God Is the Refuge of His Saints." One stanza reads:

Let mountains from their seats be hurled
Down to the deep and buried there,
Convulsions shake the solid world
Our faith shall never yield to fear.

Psalm 93 is the psalm of the floods. Three times they are mentioned. "The *floods* have lifted up, O Lord, *the floods* have lifted up their voice; the *floods* lift up their waves." But then the Psalmist says, "The Lord on high is *mightier* than many waters." Today the enemy has come in like a flood. There is a flood of pornography, a flood of V.D., a flood of stealing, a flood of divorce, a flood of broken marriages, and a flood of unbelief. So, right here we have the right to ask that the Spirit of the Lord lift up a standard against it all. He will do this through revival in the Church.

Against this flood of hell-inspired living, what has the Church to offer? It is easy to curse the darkness, but who can strike the light? Lets leave the cultists alone for a while and get our own house in order first. The so-called evangelical church is in trouble. We have had twenty-five years of massive gospel crusades, the greatest healing meetings in history, the greatest output of Christian literature ever, the greatest conferences on evangelism, the greatest outreach on radio and now projection TV that can fling pictures of so-called 'revivals' right into your living room. But at the same time we have a higher crime rate than ever, a higher rate of V.D. among the kids, a higher rate of illegitimate births, more drunks than ever, more kids on dope, and more couples crowding our divorce courts. Could it be that right now we need a mighty baptism of honesty in the Church—a mighty bending of the knees and breaking of the heart to admit that we are sleeping on the job?

Some theologians talk of this day as being a post-Christian era. Dr. John White says, "You may be wondering about the church we both love. What of her future? What will happen when freedom falls down about our ears here in the West (as it surely will do sooner or later)? How will the church survive? Certainly she will not survive in her present outward form. Certainly her whoredoms will be painfully, humiliatingly exposed." (*The Golden Cow*, p. 169)

Writing in *New Wine* magazine for February, Vol. II, No. 2, p. 21, Bob Sutton says, "Traditional Christian society as we have known it is on its deathbed. Our society is not only secular in life-style and world view, but in thought and philosophy." Now what do the believers do? Stand back and watch the humanists reshape our life-style, ban our Bibles, and drive us ashamed into the woods. Sutton goes on to say, "The testing of the church in Western society cannot be far off. Let's remember that we are entering a period when everything that can be shaken is being shaken in order that the Kingdom which cannot be shaken may remain."

A humanist says, "Using technology wisely, we can control our environment (earthquakes included), and conquer poverty . . . provide humankind with unparalleled opportunity for achieving an abundant and meaningful life." Bravo! That talk is a replay of what the Fabian Socialists were saying in pre-World War I days! Humanism abolishes God and sits around in circles in a mutual admiration society in most cases. There are some pessimists among them, however.

In *The Dust of Death*, Os Guinness gets to the root of the problem when he says, "The striptease of Western thought is exposed as a mass of tortuous, twisted tensions and contradictions, oscillations and polarizations—all stemming from the alienations of men who can explain neither themselves nor their universe.

For twenty-five years we have seen the most expensive evangelism in history and yet the surface of the Nation's sin has scarcely been scratched. Where have we erred? The Church is suspect because of her preachers! Can you imagine Noah and his family standing on the Ark the day that the world was to be flooded, clapping their hands, swinging their hips and smilingly saying to that doomed, damned world, "Something good is going to happen you, happen to you *this very day*"? Or pointing their finger at those who know not God to say with sweet assurance, "Greater is he that is in you, than he that is in the world"? Yet this is done week after week. Is it right to tell others to turn their faith loose and then have a rally to raise millions of dollars?

Here is another sample of the come-on, "You out there, let me tell you that you can have anything out of His riches in glory." And yet that evangelist has to beg for his own needs. Does the God of the radio preachers never 'come through'? God has said, "Seek *ye* first the kingdom of God and his righteousness, and all these things shall be added unto *you*." Is this truth or isn't it?

Jesus said to enter the Kingdom in this manner: "Let him deny himself, take up his cross and follow me." Radio and TV preachers, however, have changed this verse into a bargain offering. "Bring all you have and get more. Follow my teaching and you will lack for nothing."

I stagger when I read a book by three Spirit-filled men talking about a national revival without once mentioning the Holy Spirit (*Crisis America*, by George Otis, Harald Bredeson and Pat Boone). I am equally saddened when I hear Spirit-filled men interpreting John's third epistle, verse 2, mainly for material prosperity. If our average

Christian was no more healthy in body than he is in soul, the Church would have to subsidize wheelchairs. If Christians were reduced materially to the level of their soul health, they would be on welfare. I never find a pastor gloating over the spiritual might and warrior-like nature of his flock. I am sure that the main reason we do not have a national revival beginning with personal revival is that we are content to live without it.

The radio preachers suggest that revival is held up because they are not on more radio stations. TV preacher-beggars are like the horse leech of Scripture saying "more, more." Since when have men begged for God's money of widow's tithes and offerings to build tennis courts and lavish surroundings while half the world is hungry and overseas missions lack money. I am sure that we have offended a holy God by staging evangelistic meetings with Hollywood effects—fancy dressed women, fancy lighting, and costly show places in this late hour of history—for the Man born in a stable. I hear more and more people saying, "I haven't listened to him for years. He's a showman. Or he's the best singer in the Nation but the worst gospel preacher."

Read this incisive word from my friend Conrad Murrell. His book *Faith Cometh* is well worth your perusal. I quote from the book by his permission.

> *FAITH*, by which a man is justified, the great theme of the Reformation, has become a word in the mouth of ignorant religionists and unethical charlatans that bears no resemblance to the Bible doctrine. One's ears have become accustomed to hearing such terms as "seed faith" (by which you give the preacher some money, and God, in turn, makes you rich), "faith promise" (in which you "believe God" for so much to give to a religious cause, and pledge yourself to give that much), "turning your faith loose,"

and "putting God on the spot" by an act of faith. Faith, in this modern age, is a commodity which you use to work miracles with, get things for yourself, heal the sick, and raise money. It is an accessory to Christianity that is greatly to be coveted because if one can find the secret to getting it and turning it loose and using it, there is no limit to how great he can become or what he can do. Therefore, we have multitudes of preachers and writers, preaching and writing on faith. Some of them are simply overzealous, yet woefully ignorant men. Others are nothing less than (forgive me) religious pimps! They are purveyors of religious nonsense catering to the carnal lusts of unconverted men or childish Christians. The racket is enormously profitable; for while you are preaching to them on faith, and they are in the irrational excitement of the great things you are promising them, you give them an opportunity to try their faith by giving everything they have to you. By the time they find out it doesn't work, you are long gone with the money in your pockets.

All of this is wicked enough, but it is not the chief mischief. The worst thing about it is that it has fouled the waters around the very fountain of life. It has beclouded the most important subject of the Bible . . . faith. It may be well argued that love is greater than faith and that Christ is the most important person of the Bible, but the sinner has access to neither except by faith (Rom. 5:1-5). Faith is not an accessory to Christianity: It is the very quality. Four times the Bible declares the just shall live by faith (Hab. 2:4, Rom. 1:17, Gal. 3:11, Heb. 10:38). We are not justified by a "profession of faith" as modern evangelism asserts, but by a walk of faith. Faith in God is the whole life of the believer in Jesus Christ, not something he picks up on option. It is impossible to please God without it (Heb. 11:6). All his devotions, prayers, sacrifices, tears, penances, and services mean nothing until a man believes God; and the value of his work can be measured in exact proportion to how much faith in God is involved in it. "This is the work of God that ye believe on him whom he hath sent" (John 6:29). Do you desire to know what work it is that God wants you to do? Then this is it. Believe Him. Nothing else matters until you do, and when you do, you will find yourself in a work of faith. If the religious work in which you are engaged can function without the supernatural hand of God, then it requires no faith on your part and is worthless in God's sight. The Christian life begins, continues and consumates in faith. Nothing less pleases Him; and you are capable of nothing greater.

Can we have a wave of honest confession and admit that with all the fund raising and hoopla in evangelism, we have not touched the strongholds of iniquity? We have marched around the Jerichos of sin, sung and clapped our hands, but no walls have fallen down. The enemy is as strongly entrenched as ever. We sit in comfort in our pews while, at least in the downtown churches, a river of human moral filth washes the very steps of the church. Where is the wisdom of saying, "Our church broadcast reaches fifty states" when an army of lost souls passes the church while we sit indifferent to these broken, hell-bound souls? Are there no Good Samaritans left? Do we have hearts of flesh or is our inner being petrified with indifference? On the other hand, the humanists want the children to be 'liberated' from 'religious taboos.' Their hearts bleed for the children who are taught to love whatsoever things are lovely and whatsoever things are just. They suggest that there is little if any profit in Bible teaching. But the Book itself says that if the root is corrupt, the fruit will be corrupt. And even in this day of scientific wonders men still do not gather grapes from thorns or figs from thistles.

When I worked with Teen Challenge in New York City years ago, I found that atheists did not call on their arrogant unbelieving friends to help discover where their runaway children were. Nor did the rich folk ring the bosses of the night clubs to ask for a posse to search the dark corners for a daughter known to be ill and pregnant, homeless and foodless. Mad. Murray and her kind do not fund a society for the promotion of the health, education, and welfare of the lost multitudes in the Upper Amazon valley. Scorn us they may, emulate us they do not. Bound by sin themselves, how can they liberate others? How can the blind lead the blind? Does godliness pay? Let this bit of history convince you.

Max Jukes, the atheist, lived a godless life. He married an ungodly girl, and from this union there were 310 who died as paupers, 150 were criminals, 7 were murderers, 100 were drunkards, and more than half of the women were prostitutes. His 540 descendants cost the State one and a quarter million dollars.

But, praise the Lord, it works both ways! There is a record of a great American man of God, Jonathan Edwards. He lived at the same time as Max Jukes, but he married a godly girl. An investigation was made of 1,394 known descendants of Jonathan Edwards of which 13 became college presidents, 65 college professors, 3 United States senators, 30 judges, 100 lawyers, 60 physicians, 75 army and navy officers, 100 preachers and missionaries, 60 authors of prominence, one a vice-president of the United States, 80 became public officials in other capacities, 295 college graduates, among whom were governors of states and ministers to foreign countries. His descendants did not cost the state a penny. "The memory of the just is blessed" (Prov. 10:7).

CAUSTIC COMMENT FROM A COMMUNIST

The Gospel is a much more powerful weapon for the renewal of society than is our Marxist philosophy. All the same, it is we who will finally beat you. We are only a handful and you Christians are numbered by the million. But if you remember the story of Gideon and his three hundred companions, you will understand why I am right. We Communists do not play with words. We are realists, and seeing that we are determined to achieve our object we know how to obtain the means. Of our salaries and wages we keep only what is strictly necessary; we give up the rest for propaganda purposes; to this propaganda we also consecrate "all of our free time and part of our holidays."

You, however, give only a little time and hardly any money for the spreading of the Gospel of Christ. How can anyone believe in the supreme value of this Gospel if you do not practice it, if you do not spread it, and if you sacrifice neither the time nor money for it?

Believe me, it is we who will win, for we believe in our Communist message and we are ready to sacrifice everything, even our life, in order that the social justice shall triumph. But you people are afraid to soil your hands.

—From *Paix Et Liberte*, a French Communist Publication

Chapter 15

When God Gets Sick

The gladdest day in the story of human history was Resurrection morning. "Today He rose and left the dead, and Satan's empire fell." It was the gladdest day for mankind, but possibly the saddest day in the life of the Lord Jesus Christ. He had told His disciples over and over again that He would rise from the dead; that no man would take His life from Him but that He would lay it down and take it up again. They did *not* believe Him! Had they done so they would have been lined up at His grave with beaming faces crying, "My Lord and my God!"

They did not believe Him. How sad He must have been that mighty morning when He had shattered the powers of hell, when He had led captivity captive and given gifts unto men, to find as He emerged from the tomb, with a million demons behind Him mourning that mighty Resurrection, that there was no welcoming party for Him. They did not believe Him then. We do not believe Him now. The swivel chair theologians are still telling the preacher boys just how much of the Bible is true today. They are afraid of the money power boys who support them; therefore they dare not cross the paltry theological lies of their denomination lest the pickets hear them say that we are overdue for some miracle ministry and doomed unless we have heaven-born, sin-shattering, earth-shaking, heaven-filling revival.

I am tired of visiting the tombs of the prophets. The living Christ could never birth a 'dead' church. Geoffrey Bull said that some are content to guard the graveclothes, but that still leaves one burning question: Where, oh, where is he who can say, "I have seen the Lord"? When the book of the Revelation begins, Jesus is in the *midst* of the seven churches. When He speaks to the last of the seven churches, He is standing outside. Think of it! Before the New Testament is completed Jesus is knocking at the door of His own blood-purchased Church, trying to get inside! Millions of dollars have been raised 'for missions' because the preachers have said that the last Great Commission of Jesus to the Church was "go ye into all the world and preach the gospel." NOT SO! The last great word of Christ to His church was repent. A thing she would not do then and a thing most preachers fear to proclaim from their pulpits even now.

About three decades ago Dr. Edwin Orr gave us a book, *The Church Must First Repent*. I have often wondered what would have happened had the Church heeded his cry. Millions have perished since. Many of the interpreters of the Scriptures agree that the picture of the church at Laodicea is a type of the end-time church—in other words, the church of today.

The Laodiceans knew then, as we know now, that there are times when God tires of the backslidings of His people and He sends judgment upon them. How many times Israel went into captivity—and not for a weekend either but years at a time. The Church from its inception has never been without spot or wrinkle or any such thing. We have had massive theologians in centuries long gone, but we have never had the Church as numerically vast as she is today. We have never had a period when Bible knowledge was more extensive than today. We drown in a sea of interpretations. We are surfeited with millions of cassettes, books, seminars, Bible schools, seminaries, radio and TV sermons and lectures, but where, oh, where is apostolic power, apostolic purity, and apostolic piety? We are told to put on the whole armor of God. Yet the Church at this hour is more like a nursery than an armory. Do you wonder that I cry for a cessation of preaching for a month and a turn to weeping and fasting for the departed glory? Here at Laodicea the Lord has suddenly come to His temple to find it again polluted with materialism. No longer is it a house of prayer for all nations.

The Laodicean church of Revelation is like many churches today:

Self-satisfied, so it does not need to pray.

Self-sufficient, so it does not want to pray.

Self-righteous, so it cannot pray.

It seems that then as well as now the progress of the human soul is from degradation to salvation to stagnation. The Laodicean church was set in the framework of thriving industry. It had attractive natural surroundings. No doubt there were prominent, even eminent, men of the board of the church. Her coffers were filled with gold. Most likely she had compassion on the poor and gave generously to missions. Laodicean crafts were sought after. Her black wool was unique in the textile world. Her tunics were a standard of excellent wear. Her eye salves were known far and wide. Even Aristotle mentioned it. The folk enjoyed the hot springs and bathed at the famous mud baths. Jesus took all these things apart to expose her shame. How differently His holy eyes see things. How far above our thinking is His. He saw their wealth as poverty. He split wide open their pride of excellence in creature comforts.

Today Jesus still speaks through the Revelation. He says you need to buy eye salve that your near blindness may be healed. You sport your black garments, but you need to come to Him to buy white attire. You need to leave the class consciousness of being well fixed because you are at the bottom of the list spiritually. You need to pull down your barns and get poor in spirit. Your riches are cash but yet trash; you buy in the wrong market. Your values are all distorted. What you have done is borrow the world's standard of success. You made it, but at the same time grieved Him. You use His name for your house of worship, but it is destitute of eternal riches. You know power and success by the measure of your city fathers but fail to recognize the true wealth of God.

As the Savior stands at the doors of our sanctuaries, is He well pleased with what He sees? Years back the Fathers of the Church thought that God was well pleased to dwell in massive cathedrals made with hands. They spent millions of dollars in cities all over the world trying to get God to take up headquarters there while in the very shades of the monoliths bearing His holy name people died of hunger. Fortunes were spent on stained-glass windows, but they did not magnetize the Holy One of Israel.

Today we have another switch. We do not render unto Caesar what is Caesar's and unto the Lord what is His. We have gone into partnership with Caesar. We have copied Hollywood, asking help from ailing film stars, and begging the strong men of sport to give us a lift. We've even gone so far as to beg the square dancers to sing us a hymn before they quit. We have smeared His holy name with healing crusades (not all of them are false). "The 'healer' cannot operate until another offering is taken." An investigating reporter of religious operations says he has "received through the mail loads of heavenly hardware—swatches of polyester prayer clothes, vials of holy water and anointing oil, blessed buttons and 'prosperity billfolds' made of vinyl." Some of these things mentioned have a rightful place even in gospel meetings, but *not* when they have a price tag on them.

Hollywood entertainers are now exalted on TV gospel 'shows.' Hear David Wilkerson on this from his book *Hollywood Holiness*:

> Hollywood holiness is promoted by celebrities who claim to be born again but who continue to live a double life. They bounce back and forth between prayer meetings and night clubs. For a substantial fee, they perform for Christian audiences, then turn around and collect fat pay checks from gambling casinos, worldly concerts, night clubs, and drinking establishments.
>
> You find these Hollywood Christians from Nashville to Beverly Hills. They claim that Jesus has called them back into the old world so they can "be a witness." They move with great ease among the jet set; they love their association with movie stars and celebrities; they yearn for the attention and respect of other performers and high society. Yet, they also want the fellowship and respect of God's people.
>
> What a sham! What an insult to the intelligence of a holy God! The truth is, these half-in, half-out Christians are using religion in a self-serving way. And, religion is using them—to make money and draw crowds. But, no matter how big the crowds, no matter how many good things happen—it is still deadly wrong to be a mixer with the world and attempt to be a Christ-witness at the same time. He that is a friend to the world is an enemy to God.
>
> Hollywood has been enlisted to help promote certain religious TV specials. Well-known evangelists produce

programs featuring gospel preaching along with appearances by some of the most ungodly celebrities in the nation. One star appeared in a whiskey ad one week; the following week he was being advertised in the same ad with an evangelist promoting his "Christian special." What a stench in God's nostrils! What fellowship has righteousness with unrighteousness? What right do the sons of Belial and the children of the devil have appearing on the same program that purports to glorify Christ?

Saints of God, don't be deceived! It's terribly wrong! And God will not let it go on much longer. These ministers who so love the adulation and friendship of the Hollywood crowd have deceived themselves.

The One with eyes as a flame of fire saw through all the show of the Laodiceans. He sees through all our showmanship also. Joel says we are to sound an alarm in all God's holy mountain. Now is the time to do it. Christ was nauseated and disgusted with a church that bore His name but not His nature. The Church which flattered itself because of its commercial and political prowess was rejected in His sight. On the law of averages God's house today is neither a house of prayer nor a house of power. So as with Laodicea so with us, He stands outside. I ask myself each time I leave the sanctuary not what I got out of the service or what the other listeners got but what did the Lord get out of the meeting. Did He see the travail of His soul? Was He satisfied?

There's an awkward word in Exodus 28:38 where it speaks of "the iniquity of holy things." Alas many things that God ordained have become polluted. I wince when I hear the announcement of a gospel extravaganza. I shudder to think that the precious blood of Christ and His mighty work of redemption can be dulled and dirtied with the title of a fascination "Talk and Variety Show." It borders on blasphemy!

I am aware that the heart is cleansed by the blood. I think that we shall have to be corrected by the rod! I fear at times that the Nation will suffer for the sin of the Church rather than the Church suffer for the sin of the Nation. The Church needs to repent, to shed her worldliness. The preachers need to repent first. "Let the priests, the ministers of the Lord, weep before the barren altars, weep over the lost, unloved, unsought millions, weep that there is not a pillar of fire over the sanctuary, saying that God is in residence. HE stands at the door. Will He wait much longer? Let the Church live again with holy passion and America will be re-born. There is no other door of hope.

Epilogue

BE WISE

         BE WARNED

                 BEWARE

Let the heathen rage and the people imagine a vain thing.

Let iniquity abound and the love of many wax cold.

Let the seas roar and the land be shattered by earthquakes.

Let governments continue to dismantle the Ten Commandments.

Let the scoffers in or outside the "church" continue to cry:

"Where is the promise of His coming?

All things continue even as they were before."

Let the "church" continue in her worldliness.

Let hell enlarge her mouth to swallow the multitudes.

Let Communism design more subtle devices to enslave the world.

Let believers wallow in more carnality, pray less fervently, and live more worldly.

Let fat preachers parade a thin theology.

Let us now total this end mess and mass of end-time disobedience and rebellion, THEN REMEMBER THIS:

"God has allowed us to know the secret of His plan, and it is this: He purposes in His sovereign will that ALL HUMAN HISTORY SHALL BE CONSUMMATED IN CHRIST, that everything that exists in Heaven or earth shall find its perfection and fulfillment in Him. And here is *the staggering thing*—that in all which will one day belong to Him *we have been promised a share*" (Eph. 1:9-11, J. B. Phillips).